JESUS
A SHORT LIFE

D1424341

For Josh, Sophie and Josephine

JOHN DICKSON

JESUS A SHORT LIFE

Copyright © 2008 John Dickson
This edition copyright © 2012 Lion Hudson

The author asserts the moral right
to be identified as the author of this work

A Lion Book
an imprint of
Lion Hudson plc
Wilkinson House, Jordan Hill Road,
Oxford OX2 8DR, England
www.lionhudson.com
ISBN 978 0 7459 5578 0 (print)
ISBN 978 0 7459 5701 2 (e-pub)
ISBN 978 0 7459 5700 5 (Kindle)

Distributed by:
UK: Marston Book Services, PO Box 269,
Abingdon, Oxon, OX14 4YN
USA: Trafalgar Square Publishing,
814 N. Franklin Street, Chicago, IL 60610
USA: Christian Market: Kregel Publications,
PO Box 2607, Grand Rapids, Michigan 49501

First edition 2008
This edition 2012
10 9 8 7 6 5 4 3 2 1 0
First electronic edition 2012

All rights reserved

Acknowledgments

All Scripture quotations are taken from the Holy Bible, Today's New International Version, copyright © 2001, 2005 by International Bible Society. Used by permission of International Bible Society. All rights reserved worldwide. 'TNIV' and 'Today's New International Version' are trademarks registered in the United States Patent and Trademark Office by International Bible Society. Use of either trademark requires the permission of International Bible Society.

A catalogue record for this book is available from the British Library

Typeset in 11/13 Adobe Garamond Pro
Printed in Great Britain by Clays Ltd, St Ives plc

CONTENTS

Introduction

WHY THE HEADLINES ALMOST ALWAYS GET HIM WRONG

JESUS IN THE NEWS

Jesus Christ is back – if he ever went away. Back in print. Back on film. Back in the news too.

It has been nineteen centuries since the Roman statesman Tacitus denounced the 'man called Christ' whose 'deadly superstition' had found its way to Rome 'where all things hideous and shameful from every part of the world meet and become popular'.[1] And the headlines remain as colourful as ever.

Leaving aside the ubiquitous 2003 novel (and 2006 film),[2] the last few years have witnessed an unprecedented stream of blockbuster-style claims about the man from Nazareth. Believers and sceptics alike have hardly had time to process one controversial theory before the next one hits the market. First there was the National Geographic documentary extravaganza, *The Gospel of Judas* (2006), announcing to the world that a document had been uncovered purportedly written by the traditional betrayer of Jesus himself.[3] Not to be outdone, the Discovery Channel aired its own multi-million dollar TV special in early 2007. *The Tomb of Jesus* related the discovery of Jesus' family tomb in Talpiot, south Jerusalem, complete with possible DNA samples of the Son of God himself. About the same time, best-selling British novelist Jeffrey Archer paired up with Roman Catholic theologian Francis Moloney to publish

The Gospel According to Judas (nothing to do with the National Geographic documentary), a beautifully designed 'historical fiction' in which the traditional 'betrayer' of Jesus reminisces to his son about the real events surrounding the noble teacher from Galilee.[4] Most recently, the controversial US bishop John Shelby Spong entered the fray with *Jesus for the Non-Religious.*[5] This is a full-scale explanation of his long-held view that the major details of the Jesus story – his birth in Bethlehem, the names of his parents, the healings, the twelve apostles, the trial and crucifixion scenes and, of course, the resurrection – are all fictional additions to an undoubtedly significant life. The HarperCollins press release accompanying my review copy was not exaggerating when it described the Spong phenomenon as 'controversial', 'much-anticipated' and 'best-selling'.

THE ALLURE OF CONTROVERSY

I will interact with some of the details of these recent claims in the chapters that follow. For now I want to draw attention to a more significant and useful point, one that is worth holding in mind as we take a tour through the life of Christ. The most widely publicized portraits of Jesus are invariably the 'controversial' ones, those that challenge traditional perspectives. And it is easy to see why.

The announcement that Jesus' stomping ground, known as Lower Galilee, was a deeply *Jewish* part of first-century Palestine is hardly going to excite the producers of the Discovery Channel, even though it is based on solid breakthroughs in archaeological research and has convinced most experts in the field. The claim that Jesus was married to Mary Magdalene, on the other hand, and that he was buried next to her in south Jerusalem – now *that* is exciting and therefore newsworthy. It does not matter that it is based on compounding conjectures and has persuaded no serious historian.

But it is not just the fault of the media. The case of Bishop John Shelby Spong shows that even theologians feel the allure of controversy. Spong is no fool and must know how idiosyncratic his views are in academic circles, if not amongst his ecclesiastical peers. Assuming the bishop has read the chorus of scholarly criticism of the theory he relies on – known as the 'midrashic hypothesis' of the Gospels – he has judged it expedient *not* to reveal this to his readers or to acknowledge just how marginal these views are in the field of historical Jesus studies.[6]

The result of this hunger for controversy – amongst the media and some popular writers – is that the general public's perception of what experts think about the Jesus of history is massively skewed by voices from the margins of the scholarly playing field. Nowadays, the public could be forgiven for thinking that *most* scholars think *most* of the details of Jesus' life are either unknown to us or completely contrary to what Christians find in their treasured Gospels. Neither is true, as we shall see.

MARGINS AND THE MAINSTREAM

Every area of academic enquiry has its margins – science, medicine, history, law, philosophy and so on. Marginal scholars are often nay-sayers. They spend their time poking holes in the dominant theories of their discipline and chasing up loose ends in the hope of finding something exciting. Sometimes it pays off. Every now and then a marginal voice does propose a radical new way of looking at things which, while initially criticized, ends up being confirmed.

But this is the exception not the rule. Scholarship normally advances through small increments of carefully nuanced (that is, boring) pieces of research from a range of experts in the field. The findings are reviewed by peers, published in the established journals and slowly become part of the ongoing scholarly conversation. It is very, very rare, and inherently unlikely, that anything new and significant will emerge from a TV documentary or a popular-level book (such as the one you are reading now).

In historical Jesus studies, as with many other disciplines, there is a 'mainstream' and there is a 'margin'. Over the last thirty years historical scholars have inched towards something resembling a consensus about the man from Nazareth, certainly concerning the major details of his life. Even as critical a scholar as Professor Ed Sanders of Duke University, one of the leading names in the field and no friend of Christian apologetics (the defence of the faith), can write, 'There are no substantial doubts about the general course of Jesus' life: when and where he lived, approximately when and where he died, and the sort of things that he did during his public activity.'[7] Ignoring this broad consensus, controversial scholars continue to talk as if everything is up for grabs. The result, as I have said, is a serious skewing of the public's perception of what most historians think. Philip Jenkins, Professor of History and Religious Studies at Pennsylvania State University, has written an entire book on this worrying trend, entitled *Hidden Gospels: How the Search for Jesus Lost its Way.*[8]

Even someone as brilliant as Richard Dawkins can be fooled. Several times in *The God Delusion* the Oxford 'bright' (as he wants atheists to be called) suggests that Jesus' very existence is still a matter of dispute amongst experts – even though Dawkins himself generously concedes that it is *probable* that he lived.[9] This could be a rhetorical deceit, in fact designed to cast doubt over Jesus' existence, but the kinder interpretation is that Dawkins has only glanced at the margins of scholarship on Jesus. His list of authors on the topic bears this out. Had he delved a little deeper he would have discovered at least two things. Not only is Jesus' non-existence never discussed in academic literature – the way Plato's non-existence is never debated – but most experts also agree that there are, to use

Ed Sanders' words, 'no substantial doubts about the general course of Jesus' life'. The 'nouveau atheists' of our day – Richard Dawkins, Michel Onfray and Christopher Hitchens – have all tried their hand at historical criticism of Jesus and will make special conversation partners in the pages that follow. They will also amply illustrate that the gap between scholarly consensus and popular perception is sometimes very great indeed.

THE SILENCE OF THE MAINSTREAM

Meanwhile, mainstream scholars of the historical Jesus – the 80 per cent of experts who fill the more than 100 relevant peer-reviewed journals – almost never get involved in popular debate. They just busy themselves with analysing Jesus the way Roman historians study Mark Antony, Nero and Seneca, or Greek historians assess Alexander, Epictetus and Plutarch. The bulk of these experts avoid the dramatic nay-saying of the sceptical fringe as well as the overreaching arguments of Christian apologists.

For the most part, mainstream scholars simply ignore the general public. They suppose (perhaps reasonably enough) that most of us are not interested in the latest archaeological data from Lower Galilee, or the recent discovery of the Gospel of John's pool of Siloam, or the advances in our understanding of how oral histories are preserved. So, they just get on with the business of scholarship, leaving the rest of us to work it out for ourselves.

I fear things may get worse before they get better. The more airtime the controversial fringe gets, the more reticent mainstream scholars will be to get involved in discussions driven by speculation and novelty rather than the academic ideals of argument and peer review, not to mention evidence. I think I glimpsed this reticence firsthand recently in a series of TV interviews I conducted with some of the leading figures in the study of Jesus' life – whose work we will meet in the following pages. I was taken aback on several occasions by the evident suspicion many of them harboured towards popular-level productions on Jesus. It left me wondering how long it would be before the public's perception of what scholars think about Jesus corresponds to reality.

HISTORY RULES

All of this provides the background for this book. I should make clear that this is not a work of scholarship. It is intended to be an accessible and reliable *re*-presentation of what the leading historical experts are saying about the life of Jesus. The bibliography will indicate how large and varied this scholarly industry is, but I have deliberately kept notes to a minimum. Only when I suspect the average reader will want to read more on a topic or verify some unexpected claim will I bother to offer more technical references (in the Notes listed by chapter).

I should also flag that I am self-consciously limiting myself in this book. There are many more things I believe about Jesus Christ than are detailed in this small work. This is not just a matter of word-count; it has to do with my method and my aim. While Christianity is a strikingly historical religion, not everything Christians believe can be verified or even assessed by historians. And, in what follows, I am choosing to explore only what historical method can uncover and what the majority of scholars accept as probable. In other words, I am wearing my historian's hat only, not that of a theologian or even a Christian. So, for instance, I will not discuss the claim that Jesus was born of a virgin. No responsible historian can say there is anything like historical evidence for this doctrine – many simply reject it outright. I will leave this part of the Jesus story to one side. Christians reading this might interpret such an approach as 'going soft', but in fact, it is just a function of writing a historical book rather than a work of Christian apologetics. It is part of the 'rules' I have set myself. I think the average reader today wants to know not only what Christians believe to be true – an important theme I have written about elsewhere – but also what historians say can be demonstrated without recourse to theological arguments.

The presupposition that *the Bible is God's word and therefore entirely trustworthy* is perfectly arguable at the philosophical level. But it has no place in this book. To put it bluntly but no less accurately, in what follows I intend to approach the New Testament as an entirely human document, no more (*or less*) credible than the many other texts we possess from the period, such as the Jewish writings of Josephus, the Greek writings of Lucian or the Roman writings of Suetonius. Historians working on these texts agree that each of them displays bias, utilizes unreferenced sources and is capable of errors of judgement and fact. With eyes wide open to this inbuilt messiness of history, scholars have developed methods for analysing the texts in order to arrive at a plausible account of the events and people contained in them. The New Testament is no different despite its extraordinary claims. It is a text (or, rather, *collection* of texts) written at a particular point in history by historically conditioned human beings, and because so much of it has to do with purported events in the Mediterranean between 5 BC and AD 60, the New Testament invites *historical* analysis in a way that other 'holy books' do not (something my Muslim friends have frequently pointed out to me).[10]

The historian who happens to be a Christian must learn never to smuggle in religious beliefs under the guise of a historical argument. This is what separates the historian from the apologist – an honesty about what history does and does not affirm. Incidentally, the sceptic must also learn to admit when conclusions arise from disbelief rather than from historical considerations – Spong comes quickly to mind. I hope it is already obvious to readers that throughout this book I intend to maintain this historical integrity.

I will affirm as history only those things that the historical critical method can reliably establish and that the consensus of scholars affirms. The upshot of this approach (and something that may frustrate my Christian readers) is that the content of this book in no way encompasses all that I hold to be true about Jesus.

1

JESUS ON THE MARGINS OF HISTORY

History is like a game of 'joining the dots'. It is about connecting texts with artefacts with archaeological remains in an effort to piece together a plausible picture of events and people from the past. And, unfortunately, the 'dots' of history are usually unnumbered and very incomplete.

THE RANDOMNESS OF HISTORY

The historian trying to reconstruct a picture of what life was like in the ancient world faces innumerable difficulties. What has survived of the writings and buildings of, say, first-century Jerusalem, Rome or Athens would amount to the tiniest fraction of what was actually penned and constructed in the period – much less than 1 per cent. The randomness of what remains (and what does not) and what is discovered (and what is not) guarantees that what we know about the past is accidental and lop-sided. For instance, we have discovered countless shopping receipts, love notes and private letters from nobodies of the first century and yet have never found a single piece of personal correspondence from the man who ruled the world when Jesus lived: Emperor Tiberius.

ABSENCE OF EVIDENCE = EVIDENCE OF ABSENCE?

What has this got to do with Jesus? In the first place, the randomness of history – that is, the unpredictability of what survives – should caution us against assuming what kind of evidence we ought to possess for the life of Christ. A principle of historical enquiry I learnt early on in my studies states: *absence of evidence does not equal evidence of absence* (you might want to read that a couple of times). In other words, just because historians cannot find documentary or archaeological corroboration for an event or person does not mean that the event never occurred or the person never existed.

A glaring example comes to mind. In passing, the Gospel of John mentions a public pool in the district of Siloam.[1] But archaeological digs in the city had failed to discover it. Some scholars began proposing that such geographical details were fictitious, intended to be symbolic. Then, in June 2004 during sewerage works in the Siloam district of old Jerusalem, workers accidentally uncovered a huge public bath.[2] It was still being excavated when I visited the site in March 2007, but already you can see that the pool is about 50 metres (164 feet) long, with steps leading into it from all sides. It is definitively dated to the first century.[3] Imagine the scholarly embarrassment at the discovery of such a large non-metaphorical pool of Siloam.

Imagine, then, if we discovered copious amounts of correspondence between, say, Pontius Pilate, governor in Palestine at the time of Jesus, and Emperor Tiberius in Rome. Would we find a mention of Jesus in them? Perhaps. History does sometimes throw up unpredictably detailed information – notes between lovers, for example. But history is rarely obedient to expectations. I suspect that even if we were to find a batch of letters for the very year of Jesus' death (AD 30), historians would not expect to find mention of him. There were thousands of Jewish troublemakers in this period, and thousands of executions too; the chance of any one of them appearing in such randomly discovered correspondence is very small. And, as I will explain in our discussion of the crucifixion, killing Jesus was probably a very minor matter for Pilate.

JESUS WAS A 'MARGINAL JEW'

There is another point worth making. Whatever expectations we might dare to hold about the 'evidence for Jesus', logic dictates that they should start from a low base. Why? Because Jesus was a very minor figure. Even within Palestine Jesus was by no means the most famous religious figure. The movement he created – what he called the 'kingdom of God' – really amounted to just a few hundred men and women out of a total Palestinian population of about two million. Jesus himself noted the marginal nature of his movement in a parable, 'an extended metaphor or simile frequently becoming a brief narrative, generally used in biblical times for didactic purposes'[4]:

> *'What shall we say the kingdom of God is like, or what parable shall we use to describe it? It is like a mustard seed, which is the smallest of all seeds on earth. Yet when planted, it grows and becomes the largest of all garden plants, with such big branches that the birds can perch in its shade'*
> *(Mark 4:30–32).*

Humanly speaking, no one could have predicted just how large the tree Jesus planted would eventually become – today over two billion people claim to be Christians.[5] During his lifetime, though, the 'mustard seed' was a perfectly apt description of the (apparent) significance of this reputed healer and teacher from Galilee. One of the leading US scholars captures this historical reality perfectly in the provocative title of his three-volume masterpiece on the historical Jesus, *A Marginal Jew*. He notes, 'From the viewpoint of the Jewish and pagan literature of the century following Jesus, the Nazarene was at most a "blip" on the radar screen.'[6]

A 'BLIP' OR TWO ABOUT JESUS

Having said that, Jesus did cause a small handful of 'blips' on the radar screen of antiquity. He managed to get himself mentioned in no fewer than eleven texts in the Graeco-Roman writings of the first and second centuries. These are not all of equal importance, and I have written about them in more detail in another book.[7] But let me quote three of the significant ones.

Flavius Josephus (AD 37–100) was a Jewish commander in Palestine during the bloody four-and-a-half-year war with Rome, which ended in AD 70 with the destruction of Jerusalem and its holy Temple. He lived out his final years in Rome under the patronage of the emperors, and it was there that he wrote his massive *Jewish Antiquities*, a goldmine of historical information for the period. I recently had the privilege of viewing a 900-year-old manuscript of Josephus' work, which is lovingly stored in the Special Collections Library of St John's College, Cambridge. In any case, in Section 20 of *Jewish Antiquities* Josephus mentions the execution of several Jewish men in Jerusalem in the year AD 62. After a brief trial before the Sanhedrin (the Jewish court) at the direction of Ananus the high priest, the men were stoned to death as religious 'law-breakers'. Josephus' description of the event would be unremarkable if it were not for the passing mention of the *brother* of one of the victims, Jesus:

> *And so he [Ananus the high priest] convened the judges of the Sanhedrin and brought before them a man named James, the brother of Jesus who was called the Christ, and certain others. He accused them of having transgressed the law and delivered them up to be stoned. Those of the inhabitants of the city who were considered the most fair-minded and who were strict in observance of the law were offended at this.*[8]

The James mentioned here is one of four brothers of Jesus who are mentioned by name in the New Testament.[9] Our New Testament records cut off at around AD 60, when James was still alive and kicking. Josephus finishes the story off for us: James was martyred in the holy city.

Most interesting for historians is the fact that Josephus identifies James by referring to his better-known brother, Jesus, who Josephus says 'was called the Christ'. What we find here is an example of the randomness of history. We are just plain lucky that a Jewish aristocrat living in the emperor's palace in the late first century chose, for reasons unknown, to make passing reference to a relatively minor figure from Palestine decades earlier; how was Josephus to know that this man would become a central figure in Western history?

Our second example comes from around the same period (or a little earlier). Mara bar Serapion was an educated Syrian from Samosata in south-east Turkey. Writing from prison to his son, Mara warns his boy that sometimes even the wise are persecuted by the powerful. He offers three historical examples of the principle – Socrates, Pythagoras and an unnamed wise Jewish king:

> *What good did it do the Athenians to kill Socrates, for which deed they were punished with famine and pestilence? What did it avail the Samians to burn Pythagoras, since their country was entirely buried under sand in one moment? Or what did it avail the Jews to kill their wise king, since their kingdom was taken away from them from that time on? God justly avenged these three wise men. The Athenians died of famine, the Samians were flooded by the sea, the Jews were slaughtered and driven from their kingdom, everywhere living in the dispersion. Socrates is not dead, thanks to Plato; nor*

Pythagoras, because of Hera's statue. Nor is the wise king, because of the new law which he has given.[10]

There is a consensus amongst scholars that Mara bar Serapion's 'wise king' is none other than Jesus. It simply strains belief to imagine that there could have been two figures in first-century Palestine fitting the description of Jew, law-giver, king and martyr (at the hands of his own people).[11]

Finally, a leading Roman intellectual named Tacitus mentions Jesus – again in passing – in his multi-volume *Annals* of the Roman empire written between AD 114 and 117. In his account of the great fire of Rome in June AD 64 he pauses to explain where the name 'Christians' came from, since Emperor Nero tried to blame the devastation on this small religious community:

But neither human help, not imperial munificence, nor all the modes of placating Heaven, could stifle scandal or dispel the belief that the fire had taken place by order. Therefore, to scotch the rumour, Nero substituted as culprits, and punished with the utmost refinements of cruelty, a class of men, loathed for their vices, whom the crowd styled Christians. Christus, the founder of the name, had undergone the death penalty in the reign of Tiberius, by sentence of the procurator Pontius Pilatus, and the pernicious superstition was checked for a moment, only to break out once more, not merely in Judaea, the home of the disease, but in the capital itself, where all things horrible or shameful in the world collect and find a vogue.[12]

Needless to say, Tacitus was not enamoured with the 'pernicious superstition' of the Christians. The main historical importance of the passage is the evidence it provides of Roman antipathy to Christians in the time of Nero (and Tacitus), but the passing clarification about the execution of the Jew 'Christus' provides obvious corroboration for the death of Jesus during the governorship of Pontius Pilate (AD 26–36).

WHY (ALMOST) NO ONE DOUBTS JESUS' EXISTENCE

Let me conclude the chapter by saying what really should not have to be said. No one doubts the existence of Jesus. Or, perhaps more accurately, no one *in the know* doubts the existence of Jesus. Christopher Tuckett is Professor of New Testament at Oxford University (and in no sense a Christian apologist). He concludes his textbook discussion of the non-Christian sources about Jesus with these sober words:

> *All this does at least render highly implausible any far-fetched theories that even Jesus' very existence was a Christian invention. The fact that Jesus existed, that he was crucified under Pontius Pilate (for whatever reason) and that he had a band of followers who continued to support his cause, seems to be part of the bedrock of historical tradition. If nothing else, the non-Christian evidence can provide us with certainty on that score.*[13]

The Professor of the Public Understanding of Science, Richard Dawkins, may quip, 'It is even possible to mount a serious, though not widely supported, historical case that Jesus never lived at all',[14] but no one who is actually *doing history* thinks so. To describe Jesus' non-existence as 'not widely supported' is an understatement. It would be akin to my saying, 'It is possible to mount a serious, though not widely supported, scientific case that the 1969 lunar landing never happened.' There are fringe conspiracy theorists who believe such things – entire documentaries are premised on it[15] – but no expert does. Likewise with the Jesus question: his non-existence is not regarded even as a possibility in historical scholarship. Dismissing him from the ancient record would amount to a wholesale abandonment of the historical method. If a person mentioned in so many sources (both Christian and non-Christian) can turn out to be fictional, then we would have to start erasing countless other figures from the pages of the textbooks.

2

HOW HISTORIANS READ THE NEW TESTAMENT

The non-Christian evidence discussed in Chapter 1 is only part of the reason scholars are certain that Jesus walked the roads of Palestine and was crucified under Pontius Pilate. The major part of their confidence comes from the wealth of historical data found in the earliest of our sources, the evidence of the first Christians. Leaving aside Christian theology, which says the Bible is the word of God, how do historical scholars approach the texts of ancient believers? The first thing to note is that while historians do not treat the Christian writings as privileged bearers of truth, nor do they dismiss them or place them on a lower level of historical worth than any of the other Graeco-Roman texts from the period. This has to be said over and over today because somehow people have got it into their heads that a religious text, such as the New Testament, cannot be a legitimate historical text. This is not how historians approach the matter. The second thing to emphasize is that the Christian literature is not studied as *one* source at all. Even the writings of the New Testament, which appear in a single volume today, cannot be read as a unit. How could they be when they were written by different people at different times in different places? For the most part, the writers of the New Testament had no knowledge of the other texts that would end up in the volume Christians came to regard as sacred.

So, what are these varied Christian sources from the early centuries? We begin with the latest of the Christian sources.

THE GNOSTIC GOSPELS

One positive outcome of recent conspiracy theories about Christian origins is that the general public has become aware of a group of sources scholars have been working with for decades, the so-called 'Gnostic Gospels'.[1] In 1945 in the Upper Egyptian town of Nag Hammadi a large collection of ancient writings was found. Amongst the most important were thirteen codices, or ancient books, containing fifty-two separate writings produced by various Christian groups sometime between the second and fourth centuries AD. All thirteen volumes (or twelve and a bit to be precise) are stored in the Coptic Museum in Old Cairo.

The bulk of the writings betray a clear 'Gnostic' influence. From the Greek word for *knowledge*, 'Gnosticism' was a philosophical movement that insisted that the traditional story of Jesus needed to be supplemented, even supplanted, with special information secretly passed on to a select few during his lifetime: to Thomas, according to the Gospel of Thomas; to Philip, according to the Gospel of Philip; to Peter, according to the Gospel of Peter and so on. Here are just two of those secrets, taken from the Gospel of Thomas:

> *Saying no.108. He who drinks from my mouth will become like me, and I will become like him, and the hidden things will be revealed to him.*
>
> *Saying no.114. Simon Peter said to them: Let Mariham [Mary] go out from among us, for women are not worthy of the life. Jesus said: Look, I will lead her that I may make her male, in order that she too may become a living spirit resembling you males. For every woman who makes herself male will enter into the kingdom of heaven.*[2]

When you read statements like these you can begin to feel a bit of sympathy with the majority of second- and third-century Christians who ignored or despised this Gnostic material as idiosyncratic and misleading. Half a dozen sayings in the Gospel of Thomas may well be authentic – though not the two quoted above – but the overall portrait of Jesus is suspiciously non-Jewish and heavily manufactured according to Gnostic values.[3]

It is sometimes wrongly said that there were many Gospels of equal value in the early church and that it was simply a political decision later in the fourth century that included just four Gospels in the Christian New Testament. Professor Richard Dawkins rehearses this line in a recent book,[4] but the reality is that the four Gospels now in the New Testament can be shown to have been written in the first century. By contrast, all of these others come from the second or third century. This is far too long after Jesus lived to be taken seriously as historical records. Only with a fertile imagination and a neglect of the evidence can it be argued that the four New Testament Gospels were chosen 'arbitrarily' out of a larger sample of alternative (Gnostic) Gospels.[5] Historians do study the Gnostic literature for details about Christian splinter groups in the centuries after Christ, but there is not much confidence placed in these documents as sources for the historical Jesus himself.[6]

PAUL'S EPISTLES

If the Gnostic Gospels are our latest Christian sources, then some written by the apostle Paul are the earliest – and they *did* make it into the New Testament. Paul, who was also known as Saul, was a one-time persecutor of the Christians. In around AD 31–32, however, while on assignment to arrest Christians in Damascus, he encountered the one whose memory he had sought to destroy.[7] From that moment until the time of his death three decades later Paul devoted himself utterly to proclaiming what he once despised. The crucified man Jesus was, Paul now believed, God's appointed Lord of the world. He was the messiah, the Son of God.

Paul took this message not only to his fellow Jews but also, especially, to non-Jews or Gentiles. He founded communities of Christ-believers and stayed in touch with them as he travelled about by writing letters to them, answering their questions, settling disputes and constantly reminding them not to forget his 'gospel', the good news he preached to them. Only a handful of these letters has survived. They date from between AD 50 and 64, after which he was martyred in Rome.[8] These documents are not narratives of Jesus' life; they are exhortations to stay true to Jesus. The evidence they give us about Jesus is incidental but surprisingly wide-ranging. It is completely mistaken to say, as Richard Dawkins does, that the epistles of Paul 'mention almost none of the alleged facts of Jesus' life'.[9] In fact, he mentions quite a few:

- The name 'Jesus' (1 Thessalonians 1:1 and in just about every other paragraph of his letters);
- Jesus was born of a Jewish woman and was therefore a Jew himself (Galatians 4:4);
- Jesus' earthly mission focused exclusively on the Jewish people (Romans 15:8);
- Jesus had several brothers (1 Corinthians 9:5), one of whom was named James (Galatians 1:19);
- Jesus appointed a special group of twelve apostles (1 Corinthians 15:5), two of whom acquired special status, Cephas/Peter and John (Galatians 2:9);
- Jesus was called 'the Christ/Messiah' (Romans 9:3–5);
- Jesus granted his missionaries the right to material support from fellow believers (1 Corinthians 9:14);

- Jesus taught on marriage (1 Corinthians 7:10), summarized his 'law' in terms of compassion (Galatians 6:2) and declared that he would return in glory (1 Thessalonians 4:15);
- Jesus had a special last meal with his disciples involving bread and wine (1 Corinthians 11:23–25);
- Jesus was betrayed by someone on the night of the Last Supper (1 Corinthians 11:23);
- Jesus was executed by crucifixion (Philippians 2:8);
- Jesus was buried (1 Corinthians 15:4) rather than left to the elements (as convicted criminals frequently were);
- Jesus was raised to life (Romans 1:4);
- The risen Jesus appeared to many, including Peter/Cephas, his brother James and Paul himself (1 Corinthians 15:5–8).

Paul's letters were not intended to inform readers about the life of Jesus (as the Gospels clearly were); he could assume they knew all this stuff already. And *that* is the significant historical point. These writings prove that what was later written down in detail in the Gospels was already *in broad terms* being proclaimed by teachers and being committed to memory by disciples decades earlier.

With that, let me turn to the Gospels themselves.

NEW TESTAMENT GOSPELS

Paul's letters might be our earliest Christian writings, but the Gospels are universally accepted as the most important sources for understanding the life of Jesus. So, what is a 'Gospel'?

For someone like Bishop John Shelby Spong the Gospels are not news about actual events but *pious fiction* with a spiritual message. 'The concern of the gospel writers,' he insists, 'was not to record what happened in history, but to probe the experience that people had with Jesus.'[10] Such a statement will resonate with post-modern literary critics, and perhaps with a few theologians, but it will puzzle the historian who studies the Gospels in their ancient context.

Spong seems unaware of the broad consensus of scholarship that the Gospels are a particular example of the Graeco-Roman genre of *bios* or biography.[11] The *bios* was not a biography in the modern sense, in which authors explore their subjects in intimate detail from cradle to grave. It was instead a punchy, straightforward portrait of the deeds and words of great lives. All would agree that ancient biographers had an agenda in retelling the stories, but there is no question these stories were meant to be read as *real* episodes from the subject's life.

This perspective is perfectly apparent in the opening paragraph of the Gospel of Luke. He emphasizes the importance of reliable information about his subject (Jesus):

> *Many have undertaken to draw up an account of the things that have been fulfilled among us, just as they were handed down to us by those who from the first were eyewitnesses and servants of the word. With this in mind, since I myself have carefully investigated everything from the beginning, I too decided to write an orderly account for you, most excellent Theophilus, so that you may know the certainty of the things you have been taught (Luke 1:1–4).*

The reference to 'eyewitnesses' above has to be taken seriously. Unless Luke is simply lying, it is clear that at the time he was writing – in the 70s AD – the testimony of those who had actually seen and heard Jesus was valued above everything else. Recent scholarship has shown this to be a widely held view in the ancient world. People in the first century were not simpletons who believed absolutely everything they heard; they knew that reliable access to the past came principally from those who had experienced it. This was the major finding of Professor Samuel Byrskog of the University of Göteborg in his widely acclaimed *Story as History, History as Story*, published in 2002.[12] The conclusion was taken further in 2006 by Professor Richard Bauckham of the University of St Andrews. Bauckham has demonstrated the high probability that the core of the Gospels' story derives directly from those who encountered Jesus personally and that there are numerous indications of this within the books themselves.[13] The notion that the New Testament biographies of Jesus were intended as metaphorical accounts of the spiritual life has no currency amongst contemporary scholars.

SOURCES WITHIN THE GOSPELS: MARK, Q, L, SQ

In the above passage Luke also mentions the 'many' before him who had likewise written accounts of the life of Jesus. Who were these 'many'? One person, according to most scholars, was Mark, who a decade earlier wrote what we call the Gospel of Mark. A careful analysis of the Gospels of Luke and Matthew suggests that both writers used the Gospel of Mark as a basis for their own work on Jesus. There is good evidence that the Gospel of Mark relied heavily on the eyewitness testimony of the apostle Peter, one of Jesus' key disciples, so it makes sense that Matthew and Luke would both use Mark as a basis for their own account of Jesus.[14]

But Luke and Matthew did not leave it there. Scholars detect another three sources.[15] One of these they held in common. It is called Q, from the German word *Quelle* meaning *source* (not very imaginative, I know). It appears to have been a collection of Jesus' sayings and included some of the most famous ones: 'Blessed are the peacemakers', 'turn the other cheek' and so on. But how do experts know that Q existed? Large portions of

Luke and Matthew are virtually identical to each other and yet are not found in Mark. How do we explain this? It could be that Luke copied Matthew (or the other way around). But then we would face the problem of explaining why these two Gospels, in other respects, radically differ from one another. If Luke copied Matthew (or the other way around), then we would expect far more common material and shared themes. The best solution, then, in the opinion of a large majority of scholars, is to suppose that Matthew and Luke shared another source in addition to the Gospel of Mark. That source is known as Q.

No manuscript of Q has ever been found but its assumed existence is well founded. It is the same logic I would apply if two of my students handed in essays with identical wording in a number of their paragraphs. There are two options. Either one has copied the other or they have both *independently* used another source, perhaps a textbook or (more likely nowadays) a web page. If the essays argued in a similar fashion and came to the same conclusions, then I would probably assume that one had copied from the other. But if, despite the identical paragraphs, the bulk of the essays differed substantially, then I would probably conclude that the students had relied on a shared source. Even if I could not actually identify that source – just as scholars cannot produce a manuscript of Q – the existence of it is still the best explanation. Hence, throughout this book I will frequently say things like, 'In a passage from Q Jesus says…' This does not mean I have found the elusive document; it is the standard scholarly way of referring to passages found only in Matthew and Luke and which (very probably) come from a source they held in common.

The other two sources are known as 'L' and 'M'. These are not shared sources like Q. 'L' stands for a source unique to Luke's Gospel and 'M' for one unique to Matthew's Gospel. But if these are not shared sources, how on earth do we know they existed? Again, nothing is certain, but there is a real logic to it (scholars rarely invent complexities just for the sake of it). In Luke's Gospel there is a lot of material that comes neither from Mark nor from Q; it is unique to his Gospel. So where did it come from? It is possible he just invented it, but the reality is that much of this unique material has a common literary style that is noticeably different from Luke's own writing style. There are plenty of places in this Gospel in which Luke himself writes as narrator – in much the same way as a voice-over leads viewers through a TV documentary. We thus know the way Luke likes to write: he has a particular vocabulary and grammatical style. But some portions of this Gospel display *another* style, which scholars ascribe to a separate source that Luke used – just as he used Mark and Q. This is 'L'.

Matthew's source, 'M', is not as easily identifiable as 'L'. Scholars tend to be a little more uncertain about whether it was ever a *written* source; it could just as easily have been a collection of stories and sayings rehearsed *orally* in the churches known to Matthew, which he was the first to put into writing. We need to remember that the early Christians preserved the sayings and deeds of Jesus the way most communities in the ancient world maintained their most treasured cultural and ritual traditions – not through writing but through 'oral tradition'. In a day when only 10–15 per cent of the population could read, written sources were of limited value. Far more trusted were the age-old methods of memorization and transmission known as oral tradition. This is a significant area of scholarly research today, and I will refer to it from time to time throughout the book.[16]

To round things off I should probably mention that most scholars believe that the Gospel of John used its own source, called 'SQ', or *Semeia Quelle*, the Signs Source, a collection (probably written) of miracle stories that John used as a key to his narrative. John does not appear to have used any of the sources mentioned above. For reasons unknown to us, his is a rather independent Gospel.

I know this is a bit complicated. For those who just want a summary, the table below provides a brief recap of our list of Christian sources, organized roughly from the earliest to the latest.

Source	Date	Character
Paul's letters	AD 50–64	Very early testimony to the core of the Jesus story.
Q	40–70	An early collection of Jesus' teachings used by Matthew and Luke.
L	40–70	An early collection of parables and stories of Jesus used by Luke.
SQ	70	A collection of miracle stories used by John.
Gospel of Mark	65–70	Our first complete Gospel, penned as a record of the apostle Peter's testimony.
M	40–80	A collection of parables and teachings of Jesus used by Matthew.
Gospel of Luke	75–85	The second Gospel to be written, employing Mark, Q and L.
Gospel of Matthew	80–95	The third Gospel to be written, employing Mark, Q and M.
Gospel of John	80–100	The last of our first-century Gospels, employing the Signs Source, SQ.
Gnostic Gospels	120–300	The product of second-century Gnostics in reaction to the traditional Gospels. The Gospel of Thomas may contain half a dozen authentic sayings.

HISTORY AND THE CHRISTIAN SOURCES

Gnostic Gospels aside, these sources form the basis of all scholarly discussion about the historical Jesus. While the non-Christian writings discussed earlier receive some treatment in academic research, it is the Gospels (with their various sources), as well as the letters of Paul, that provide the principal data for the thousands of books and articles written on Jesus.

Of particular importance is the way a knowledge of these sources allows the historian to apply what is called the *criterion of multiple attestation*, a fundamental building block of all historical enquiry. What this means is that within the New Testament itself we can find multiple independent testimonies to various aspects of Jesus' life. That may sound counter-intuitive if you are used to thinking of the Bible as one book. But historians ignore the book binding and critically analyse the independent sources within. When some aspect of Jesus' life or teaching appears in, say, Mark and Q, or Q and Paul, or any other combination of independent sources, we have *multiple attestation*, different witnesses corroborating (without collusion) certain features of the life of Jesus.[17] It is the same logic you apply when you hear some surprising news. If it comes from one friend, you might accept it on face value. If it comes from several friends, and you know they have not colluded, you are very likely to trust what they say. It is partly on this basis – and on various other historical criteria we will meet along the way – that the broad narrative of Christ's life is not in dispute amongst mainstream scholars. Professor Graham Stanton of the University of Cambridge sums it up nicely: 'While certainty often eludes us, we do know a good deal about Jesus of Nazareth.'[18]

In the following chapter we will begin to unpack that 'good deal' we know about Jesus.

3

VITAL STATISTICS

Our historical biography of Jesus should begin with some vital statistics. When and where was he born? Where did he grow up? And what do we know of his family and trade?

WHEN EXACTLY WAS ANNO DOMINI?

You might have thought the date of Jesus' birth was a no-brainer – was he not born in the year AD 1? Unfortunately, things are not so simple.

The Gospels of Matthew and Luke agree that Jesus was born while Herod the Great, the Rome-appointed king over Palestine, was still alive. Matthew puts it plainly: 'After Jesus was born in Bethlehem in Judea, during the time of King Herod, Magi from the east came to Jerusalem.'[1] According to firm dates provided by Josephus, we know that Herod ruled from 37 BC until his death in early 4 BC.[2] So, Jesus must have been born sometime before 4 BC.

But how long before Herod's death was Jesus born? Matthew implies it was not more than about two years, which brings us to anywhere between 6 and 4 BC. Luke provides another piece of the puzzle. He says that in 'the fifteenth year of the reign of Tiberius Caesar' Jesus was 'about thirty years old'.[3] Tiberius was emperor from AD 14 to 37, so his fifteenth year was approximately AD 28. Counting backwards thirty years or so could take us to 6 BC at the limit (assuming that anything beyond thirty-four years starts to strain the description '*about* thirty years'). All of this leads to the broad consensus amongst scholars that Jesus was born around 5 BC.

Naturally, that raises the question: how could Jesus have been born five years '*before* Christ'? The answer is simple. The man who proposed the calendar distinction between BC[4] and AD (AD stands for *Anno Domini* or 'in the year of the Lord') was an Italian mathematician, archivist and theologian named Dionysius Exiguus, whose name translates as 'Denis the Little' or, as one scholar quips, 'Denny the Dwarf'.[5] In AD 525 Pope St John asked Denis to prepare a chronology based on the historical records at his disposal. Sifting through the available documents Denis calculated what he thought was the most likely 'year of the Lord'. It was then proposed that the Western/Christian calendar should reflect this determination.

It turns out that Dionysius missed the mark by a number of years. Given the limited historical data he had to work with, I think he did rather well. We now know the exact dates of figures such as Herod the Great and Emperor Tiberius, so we can confidently place Jesus' birth about five years earlier than previously thought; that is, in around 5 BC.

O LITTLE TOWN OF BETHLEHEM

Matthew and Luke both place Jesus' birth in Bethlehem.[6] Many doubt this detail, believing it to be a pious piece of 'place dropping'. Ancient King David (1000 BC) was from Bethlehem and the Gospel writers, so it is thought, wanted to associate their Lord with Israel's greatest monarch. In a glaring overstatement Bishop Spong writes, 'Was Jesus born in Bethlehem, the city of David? The answer is a very simple "no". There is almost no possibility that this claim is a fact of history.'[7] His argument is twofold: first, the Gospels of Mark and John make no mention of Jesus being born in Bethlehem and, second, because one Old Testament prophecy says that Israel's messiah would come from Bethlehem (Micah 5:2) the Gospels had to place him there to make him look messianic.

But things are not that simple. Just as important as the fact that Bethlehem is not mentioned in Mark or John is the fact that it *is* mentioned in Luke and Matthew. Surely, the silence of two of the Gospels cannot be louder than the affirmation of the other two, especially when we know that Luke and Matthew wrote independently of each other. In addition, that John and Mark say nothing about Jesus' birth in Bethlehem may actually neutralize Spong's second argument. Obviously, two of the Gospel writers felt no need to place their messiah in Bethlehem. So, what is the evidence that Matthew and Luke put him there out of some necessity to make him look messianic? None. The argument dissolves.

One cannot prove that Jesus was born in Bethlehem. Historically speaking, it is difficult to decide one way or the other. This is exactly the conclusion of the most important study of the topic to date, Professor Raymond Brown's *The Birth of the Messiah*.[8] Certainly, Christians should feel no embarrassment about the issue. Their beliefs about Jesus' birth might not be verifiable by historical method but neither are they diminished by it.

What cannot be doubted is that Jesus grew up not down south in Bethlehem but up north in Galilee.

GALILEE THE BEAUTIFUL

More than once have I heard it argued that the world's three great monotheistic faiths – Judaism, Islam and Christianity – invented their hope for a 'paradise beyond' as a way of coping with the misery of their desert origins. Who wouldn't fantasize about heavenly bliss if all they had before them was the dreary wilderness of Sinai, the endless sands of Arabia and the wasteland of Galilee? I will leave it to Jews and Muslims to point out the illogic of this argument in connection with their own origins, but in the case of Christianity this line of reasoning amounts to a real ecological blunder.

Jesus was raised in one of the most beautiful places I have ever visited. You might have your own mental images of Jesus' stomping ground, perhaps based on biblical tales of desert wanderings or the barren hills of Monty Python's *The Life of Brian*. I am meant to be an expert in this stuff and frankly I was amazed at what I saw when I first landed there. Far from being a desert, Galilee is a highly fertile region made up of rolling hills, stark mountains and a large valley leading down to the beautiful inland sea known as Lake Gennesareth or simply Lake Galilee (12 km/7½ miles wide by 20 km/12½ miles long). The lake has always provided plenty of fish for food and trade. It was by far the richest and most populous region of all ancient Palestine.[9]

I had the enormous privilege of being shown around parts of Galilee by Professor Sean Freyne of Trinity College Dublin, one of the leading experts on the region.[10] As we looked over the first-century town of Gamla with the lake in the distance I was struck by the rich green of the grass, the bright yellow of the flowers and the abundant bird life all around. We could have been in the Scottish Highlands. The idea that Christianity's hope for 'the kingdom of heaven' was fuelled by its desert origins is as false as it is facile. The first followers of Jesus, all of them Galileans like their leader, lived in a place brimming with the produce of the earth. Professor Freyne wonders if this might explain the frequent references in Jesus' teaching to flora and agriculture:

> *'Look at the birds of the air; they do not sow or reap or store away in barns, and yet your heavenly Father feeds them. Are you not much more valuable than they? Can any one of you by worrying add a single hour to your life? And why do you worry about clothes? See how the flowers of the field grow. They do not labour or spin. Yet I tell you that not even Solomon in all his splendour was dressed like one of*

> *these. If that is how God clothes the grass of the field, which is here today and tomorrow is thrown into the fire, will he not much more clothe you – you of little faith?' (Q: Matthew 6:26–30 | Luke 12:24–28).*[11]

> *'By their fruit you will recognize them. Do people pick grapes from thornbushes, or figs from thistles? Likewise, every good tree bears good fruit, but a bad tree bears bad fruit. A good tree cannot bear bad fruit, and a bad tree cannot bear good fruit. Every tree that does not bear good fruit is cut down and thrown into the fire. Thus, by their fruit you will recognize them' (Q: Matthew 7:16–20 | Luke 6:43–44).*

This is not to say that life was a breeze or that Jesus and his followers lived in the lap of luxury; far from it. Seasons could be variable, crops could fail and imperial taxes could be increased at any moment. There was also the threat of clashes with local bandits and with the occupying Romans – and Galilee had more than its fair share of those.[12]

JESUS' PARENTS

We turn from Jesus' land to his family. Bishop Spong's thoroughgoing scepticism leads him in a recent book to suggest that even the names of Jesus' parents, Joseph and Mary, are pious additions, 'fictionalized composites' he calls them, designed to evoke memories of famous Old Testament characters with the same names: Joseph of 'technicolour dream coat' fame and Miriam (Mary) who was the sister of Moses.[13] On these grounds we could reject the name 'Jesus' itself, since it was also held by the man who led Israel into the promised land (Joshua = Jesus). But the scepticism is misplaced, and most experts concur with Professor John Meier of the University of Notre Dame, the author of the acclaimed three-volume *A Marginal Jew*: 'the identification of Mary and Joseph as mother and putative father is secure'.[14]

Mary features numerous times in the Jesus story. She is there in the middle of his career in Galilee, trying to get word to him through the crowds of people flocking to hear him.[15] She is there at the end too. She witnessed his crucifixion and, afterwards, she joined with the first Christians in Jerusalem to worship God in the name of the risen Jesus.[16] Joseph, on the other hand, never appears in Jesus' adult ministry. One could speculate endlessly about the reasons for this but the oldest explanation remains the most likely. Joseph probably died sometime before Jesus launched out on his public ministry.[17] This would explain the curious fact in the Gospel of Mark that even his hometown crowd referred to Jesus not as the 'son of Joseph' but as the 'son of Mary':[18]

> *'Where did this man get these things?' they asked. 'What's this wisdom that has been given him? What are these remarkable miracles he is performing? Isn't this the carpenter? Isn't this Mary's son and the brother of James, Joseph, Judas and Simon? Aren't his sisters here with us?' (Mark 6:2–3).*

This passage is interesting for another reason. It introduces to us Jesus' siblings.

JESUS' SIBLINGS

In teaching short courses on the life of Jesus over the years I have had numerous people – not just religious folk – pipe up at this point and say, 'Hang on! What do you mean Jesus had siblings; I thought Mary was meant to have remained a virgin all her life?' This reaction is very common, so let me try to explain things as clearly as I can, without at all wanting to step on religious toes.

We met one of Jesus' brothers in Chapter 1 when we discussed the statement of Josephus: 'And so he [Ananus the high priest] convened the judges of the Sanhedrin and brought before them a man named James, the brother of Jesus who was called the Christ.'[19] However, Mark 6:2–3 (opposite) reveals the full extent of Jesus' family. He apparently had four brothers – James, Joseph, Judas and Simon – and at least two sisters (indicated by the plural).

It is possible to interpret these siblings as *step*-brothers/sisters or even as cousins, but the vast majority of scholars today – including Roman Catholic historians – acknowledge that the relevant passages most likely refer to true siblings.[20] Like most people in the period, Jesus came from (what we would regard as) a large family, at least nine in all. Only later, in the second to fourth centuries, was the idea of Mary's perpetual virginity proposed and accepted by some Christians.[21]

But more striking than the mere existence of Jesus' nine-member household is the fact that all or most of his brothers became leaders of the early Christian movement. James would go on to write one of the letters now in the New Testament; it is called simply James.[22] Moreover, he presided over the sizeable 'mother church' in Jerusalem. If you were to ask mid-first-century Christians from anywhere in the Roman empire, 'Who is the earthly figurehead of Christianity?' they almost certainly would have said, 'James, the brother of the Lord.'[23]

Jesus' other brothers (Joseph, Judas and Simon) became travelling Christian missionaries. 'Don't we have the right,' asks the apostle Paul in the mid-50s, 'to take a believing wife along with us, as do the other apostles and the Lord's brothers and Cephas?'[24] It is a lovely picture. Unlike James, who stayed in Jerusalem, the other brothers of Jesus decided to spread their faith – faith in their own brother – far and wide, and they did so in the company of their wives.[25]

DID JESUS MARRY?

Jesus' brothers had wives – but did he?

It has become fashionable in recent years – amongst popular writers rather than scholars – to claim not only that Jesus had a wife (and children) but also that we know her name: Mary Magdalene, who appears in the Gospels as a faithful disciple and supporter of Jesus.[26]

The evidence for Jesus' marriage amounts to one paragraph in the late second- or early third-century Gospel of Philip, one of the Gnostic Gospels stored in the Coptic Museum of Cairo. The relevant passage reads:

> *The S[aviour lov]ed [Ma]ry Mag[da]lene more than [all] the disciples, and kissed on her [mouth] often. The other [disciples]... [ ]. They said to him: 'Why do you love her more than all of us?' The Saviour answered and said to them [ ]: 'Why do I not love you like her?'*[27]

The bracketed parts of the above quotation indicate sections of the manuscript (written in Coptic) that are illegible or missing. I held this page in my hands when I was in Egypt recently, and there is a large hole in the bottom right corner of the manuscript where these words appear. The letters and words in the bracketed sections above indicate scholars' best guesses at what was in the original text, though this is not always possible.

I quote this passage because it is the only historical text from which it has been argued – in a novel, mind you – that Jesus married Mary Magdalene and had children with her. And, as you can see, the text says nothing of the sort; all we get is a 'kiss'.

More disappointing for those of us who quite like the idea of *Jesus the husband* is that scholars actually think the reference to 'kissing' here is religious, not romantic. Kissing fellow believers was widely practised in early Christianity, as evidenced in the New Testament itself.[28] And what are we to make of the disciples' jealousy over Mary? Can this be romantic? Hardly. They are jealous that she is the preferred disciple, not lover! It is highly doubtful that the Gospel of Philip has any basis in history – it was written about 150 years after Jesus' death – but even if it did, the point being made in the passage is not that Jesus and Mary were 'an item'; it is simply that Mary was the ideal disciple to whom other disciples should aspire. Romance, let alone marriage, is nowhere to be found.

Marriage was highly regarded amongst ancient Jews, but plenty of other Jews gave up this gift in order to perform special services to God.[29] Even in the Old Testament the prophet Jeremiah abstained from having a wife as a sign of Israel's doom.[30] Jesus may well have fitted into such a tradition, forfeiting the blessing of a wife in order to pursue his unique goal.[31]

THE CARPENTER

What Jesus did between 5 BC and AD 28 is unknown. It is tempting to call this period 'the mystery years', and some have tried to fill in the gaps with speculation about travels to Egypt to learn magic or a sojourn to India to learn from the Hindu or Buddhist seers. Over the years I have been asked numerous times about the evidence for Jesus' exotic journeys. The 'evidence' amounts to precisely nothing – which, of course, provides fertile ground for any theory.[32]

In all probability, Jesus simply grew up in his close-knit village of Nazareth with a thousand or more extended family and friends. He would have worked all week, most likely in his father's business, and attended synagogue on the Sabbath, where he would have learnt the Scriptures of Israel. Work and study were key virtues in Jewish life, and fathers were expected to teach their sons a trade as well as train them in the biblical traditions.[33]

Jesus' work, like that of his father, was almost certainly carpentry. This is mentioned only in Mark's Gospel.[34] But because nothing is made of it – no symbolism or honour is attached to the trade – scholars accept the reference as a straightforward report of a well-known detail.[35] Jesus' brothers lived on into the 50s and 60s AD, so the family business must have been public knowledge when Mark wrote his Gospel.

The word used to describe Jesus' trade (*tektōn*) means more than just a 'carpenter' in the modern sense of someone who specializes in building and repairing wooden structures, usually houses. An ancient *tektōn* fashioned the full range of objects needed in antiquity, including furniture, doors, locks, chests, ploughs, yokes and various other tools, as well as dwellings. It was tough work and required an array of skills. As Professor John Meier of the University of Notre Dame notes:

> *… he plied a trade that involved, for the ancient world, a fair level of technical skill. It also involved no little sweat and muscle power. The airy weakling often presented to us in pious paintings and Hollywood movies would hardly have survived the rigors of being Nazareth's tektōn from his youth to his early thirties.*[36]

In any case, around the age of thirty-three this single *tektōn* from Nazareth launched out onto the wider Palestinian scene as a teacher. And the world would never be the same again.

4

MENTOR AND COMPETITORS

Jesus was a teacher. A more obvious statement could hardly be made about him. Ask anyone, anywhere, what they know of the man from Nazareth and 'teaching' will probably top the list. 'Turn the other cheek', 'love thy neighbour', 'judge not lest you be judged', 'do unto others as you would have them do unto you', 'you are the salt of the earth' and a host of other expressions have attained proverbial status in Western culture, and all of them began as utterances of Jesus on the fertile hills of Galilee or in the bustling public squares of Jerusalem. Academic volumes are dedicated to the discussion of Jesus as teacher.[1] Mahatma Gandhi ranked the Sermon on the Mount – the words of Christ recorded in Matthew 5–7 – as one of the most sublime speeches in history, admitting in his autobiography, 'it goes straight to my heart'.[2] Even Richard Dawkins believes that the sayings of Jesus (and other biblical greats) ought to be studied in the classroom – for their literary significance only, of course.[3] Jesus the teacher looms large.

But in his day, Jesus was just one of a vast number of teachers. Indeed, before he launched out with his revolutionary message, he himself was probably a student of at least one teacher we know about.

JOHN THE BAPTIST

Jesus as a teacher is taken for granted. What is less well known – but on a moment's thought perfectly obvious – is that Jesus himself was once a student. Every good teacher was once taught, and Jesus was no exception. We begin our exploration of Jesus' teaching, then, with an account of his probable mentor, John the Baptist.

Many of those acquainted with the story of Jesus will know John the Baptist as the odd man at the beginning of the Gospels who lived in the desert, ate locusts and wild honey and heralded the arrival of his relative and superior, Jesus Christ. The classic passage is in Mark's Gospel (repeated in Matthew and Luke):

> *And so John the Baptist appeared in the wilderness, preaching a baptism of repentance for the forgiveness of sins. The whole Judean countryside and all the people of Jerusalem went out to him. Confessing their sins, they were baptized by him in the Jordan River. John wore clothing made of camel's hair, with a leather belt around his waist, and he ate locusts and wild honey. And this was his message: 'After me comes the one more powerful than I, the thongs of whose sandals I am not worthy to stoop down and untie. I baptize you with water, but he will baptize you with the Holy Spirit' (Mark 1:4–8; Luke 3:2–16; Matthew 3:4–6).*

But John is not just an obscure character at the start of the Gospel story; he was an important figure in ancient Palestine in his own right – important enough to receive special mention in the writings of the first-century historian Josephus. In Section 18.109–115 of *Jewish Antiquities,* Josephus blames a failed military campaign of Herod Antipas (son of Herod the Great and tetrarch, or governor, of Galilee during Jesus' lifetime) on his recent treatment of a certain holy man named John, the baptizer:

> *But to some of the Jews the destruction of Herod's army seemed to be divine vengeance, and certainly a*

> *just vengeance, for his treatment of John, surnamed the Baptist. For Herod had put him to death, though he was a good man and had exhorted the Jews to lead righteous lives, to practise justice towards their fellows and piety towards God, and so doing to join in baptism. In his view this was a necessary preliminary if baptism was to be acceptable to God. They must employ it not to gain pardon for whatever sins they committed, but as a consecration of the body implying that the soul was already thoroughly cleansed by right behaviour. When others too joined the crowds about him, because they were aroused to the highest degree by his sermons, Herod became alarmed. Eloquence that had so great an effect on mankind might lead to some form of sedition, for it looked as if they would be guided by John in everything that they did.*[4]

THE MEANING OF BAPTISM

Baptism, from the Greek word meaning 'to dip', was a Jewish ritual symbolizing a cleansing before God; it was a spiritual bath. John was not the first to appropriate the symbol. Similar washings were practised at Qumran, where the Dead Sea Scrolls were found. The Essenes who lived there washed themselves daily in purpose-built ritual baths called *mikvaot* (they are still there to this day). Another wilderness preacher named Bannus is also known to have used frequent water rituals.[5] But John added one significant new idea: his baptism was once-off. The 'baths' of Bannus and the Essenes were regular rituals – daily even. They were a perpetual reminder of the contaminations of the world and the need for divine cleansing. John, on the other hand, seems to have intensified the meaning and thereby transformed the symbol: he called people to a decisive moment of renewal marked by baptism.

What drove the immediacy in John's message and baptism was his conviction that a great disaster was about to fall on Israel if the nation did not turn back to God – or 'repent', to use the biblical language. A passage in the early Gospel source behind Matthew and Luke (known as Q) puts things very starkly:

> *But when he saw many of the Pharisees and Sadducees coming to where he was baptizing, he said to them: 'You brood of vipers! Who warned you to flee from the coming wrath? Produce fruit in keeping with repentance. And do not think you can say to yourselves, "We have Abraham as our father." I tell you that out of these stones God can raise up children for Abraham. The axe is already at the root of the trees, and every tree that does not produce good fruit will be cut down and thrown into the fire' (Matthew 3:7–10 | Luke 3:7–9).*

For John, a climactic judgement – described here as an 'axe' and a 'fire' – is likely to fall upon Israel at any moment. And so people must decide *now* to return to their Maker and seek his cleansing and renewal. They must 'repent', a word with negative modern connotations but which simply means *decide to change.*[6] Baptism, of a once-off kind, was a powerful marker of this decision.

THE MEANING OF JESUS' BAPTISM

So, where did Jesus fit into John's orbit? Scholars generally agree that Jesus emerged onto the public scene only after a period of close association with John the Baptist.[7] It may be too much to say that he was a 'disciple' of John in the strict sense but, of all the Jewish teachers active in Palestine in the period, it does seem that the Baptist was the one Jesus most admired and identified with before he launched his own mission to Israel.[8] Professor Paula Fredriksen of Boston University describes the scholarly consensus best when she says, 'What we do know past doubting is that John had a crucially important impact on Jesus.'[9]

The crucial fact here – doubted by no one doing historical Jesus research – is that Jesus publicly submitted himself to John's defining ritual. In the words of Mark's Gospel, 'At that time Jesus came from Nazareth in Galilee and was baptized by John in the Jordan.'[10] For Christians Jesus' baptism by John is such a well-known feature of the Gospel story that few pause to think what it must have meant at the time. It suggests (at the very least) that Jesus saw the Baptist's particular vision of life as the starting point and launching pad for his own preaching.

Jesus even inherited John's practice of baptism. Everyone knows that the Christian church has baptized people ever since its foundation. Less well known is the fact that this ritual – in its once-off form – comes directly from John the Baptist and, for a time, was even part of Jesus' own ministry.[11] We see here the concrete influence of the Baptist on Jesus. Also interesting is the fact that at least two of Jesus' own disciples came originally from the circle of John's disciples. This underlines the very real overlap between Jesus and John, as the apprentice becomes a master in his own right.[12]

Much of Jesus' ministry maintains the emphases of John the Baptist: his continuation of the baptism ritual, his frequent warnings of imminent judgement, his passionate plea that people return to their Maker and his promise of God's forgiveness for those who repent. All of these reflect the earlier teachings of John. It is because of this that most academic volumes on the life of Jesus devote considerable space to the study of the Baptist.[13]

But Jesus was no carbon copy of John; far from it. A passage from the early Gospel source known as Q tells us that John looked to Jesus as the promised redeemer of Israel, euphemistically called the 'Coming One'.[14] In another statement of the Baptist quoted previously, independently attested in two sources, we learn of his deference to the Coming One: 'After me comes the one more powerful than I, the thongs of whose sandals I am not worthy to stoop down and untie. I baptize you with water, but he will baptize you with the Holy Spirit.'[15] Another passage from Q reveals one obvious way in which Jesus and John differed greatly from one another. Whereas John wandered in the wilderness living as an ascetic, Jesus toured the towns and villages, eating and drinking with all and sundry – and both men were criticized for their behaviour by the establishment. As Jesus once complained:

> *'For John the Baptist came neither eating bread nor drinking wine, and you say, "He has a demon." The Son of Man [that's Jesus] came eating and drinking, and you say, "Here is a glutton and a drunkard, a friend of tax collectors and sinners"' (Luke 7:33–35 | Matthew 11:19).*

But any differences between Jesus and his mentor pale into insignificance as we turn to look at his disagreements with the mainstream teachers of his day. When Jesus launched out on his own – outside the sphere of John the Baptist – his critique of Israel's revered rabbis would amount to something of a revolution.

THE PHARISEES

In the century or two before Jesus a group arose in Israel that stressed the need for personal purity in the affairs of ordinary life. Members of the faction saw themselves as a reform movement more than a political party. They came to be known as 'Pharisees', probably from the Hebrew word *parash*, meaning 'to separate' – separated from what is impure.[16] We meet the Pharisees countless times in the life of Jesus. In a very real sense, they were his chief competitors for the hearts and minds of Galilee.

Our first-century Jewish writer, Josephus, who claimed to be a Pharisee, describes them as 'the most accurate interpreters of the laws'.[17] The statement is important. In emphasizing individual purity the Pharisees developed intricate rules concerning the affairs of daily existence – how you ate, how you washed, how and when you worked, with whom you could associate, how much of your possessions you gave to God and so on. These laws came to be known as the 'traditions of the elders' because they had been passed down from generation to generation. Jesus appears to have rejected many of these 'traditions of the elders'.

The two most famous Pharisees of the period – even more famous than Jesus – were Hillel and Shammai. Both men died shortly before Jesus began his preaching but their legacy continued for many years to come. They established long-lasting 'schools', and their teachings are still regarded as sacred by Orthodox Jews today. Shammai was said to be the stricter of the two when it came to ethical and ritual matters. He is reported to have insisted, 'Make your learning of Torah [i.e., God's instruction] a fixed obligation. Say little and do much.'[18] Rabbi Hillel, on the other hand, characterized his Judaism as the pursuit of peace and love: 'Be disciples of Aaron, loving peace and pursuing peace, loving people and drawing them near to the Torah.'[19] He also ruled that 'spoiling your dinner' was just grounds for divorcing your wife. He was quite a 'liberal' (and Jesus would have strong words to say about this matter).[20]

JESUS' DIRTY HANDS

In numerous places in the Gospels – and across the range of the sources – we find Jesus daringly challenging the intelligentsia of his day. Here he is, for example, in full flight against the Pharisees on the traditional Jewish theme of ritual hand-washing:

> *The Pharisees and some of the teachers of the law who had come from Jerusalem gathered around Jesus and saw some of his disciples eating food with hands that were defiled, that is, unwashed… So the Pharisees and teachers of the law asked Jesus, 'Why don't your disciples live according to the tradition of the elders instead of eating their food with defiled hands?' He replied, 'Isaiah was right when he prophesied about you hypocrites; as it is written: "These people honour me with their lips, but their hearts are far from me. They worship me in vain; their teachings are merely human rules." You have let go of the commands of God and are holding on to human traditions' (Mark 7:1–8).*[21]

On a recent trip to Jerusalem I was struck by the many public facilities throughout the city designed to preserve these very 'traditions of the elders'. The toilets by the famous Wailing Wall – the western wall of the ancient Temple complex – have ritual bowls chained to the wash basins for just this purpose. At first I was puzzled: they looked like large drinking mugs. Then I saw an Orthodox Jew fill a bowl with water and begin to pour it over his hand in a very precise way. He was fulfilling the ancient requirement stipulated by the 'elders'. The details are recorded in the second holy book of Judaism (after the Tanakh or Old Testament), the Mishnah. The Mishnah is the collection of the 'traditions of the elders' preserved and practised by the Pharisees between 50 BC and AD 200. The rulings about hand-washing are found in the chapter called *Yadayim*, 'hands':

> *The hands are susceptible to [spiritual] uncleanness and are rendered clean up to the wrist. How so? If one poured the first water [of two compulsory cleansings] up to the wrist, and the second beyond*

> *the wrist and it went back to the hand – it is clean. If he poured out the first and the second pouring of water beyond the wrist and it went back to the hand, it is unclean. If he poured out the first water onto one hand, and was reminded and poured out the second water onto both hands, they are unclean. If he poured out the first water onto both hands and was reminded and poured out the second water onto one hand, his hand, which has been washed twice, it is clean. If he poured out water onto one hand and rubbed it on the other, it is unclean.*[22]

From the Jewish point of view, such washings are not just symbols of devotion to God; they make one ritually 'clean' and therefore able to exist (eat, work and play) in God's holy presence. Rabbi Shammai and Rabbi Hillel both endorsed such traditions.[23] Jesus rejected them. He thought they were empty 'human traditions' obscuring the true 'commands of God'.

When you read Jesus' criticisms of the teachers in his day and imagine crowds of ordinary Jews being persuaded by him, it becomes easy to imagine why the Jewish leadership would reject this teacher from Nazareth. This is even easier to envisage when we realize that, just like his mentor John the Baptist before him, Jesus warned of judgement upon Israel.

5

KINGDOM OF JUDGEMENT AND LOVE

'Gentle Jesus, meek and mild' begins the 1742 hymn of Charles Wesley. I understand what he was getting at – there are moments of profound tenderness in Jesus' career – but if we were sitting in one of Jesus' audiences on the hills or shores of Galilee in the late 20s AD I doubt very much that these would be the first words to come to mind to describe the electrifying speaker before us.

There is a tendency in pop culture – and sometimes in scholarship – to domesticate Jesus, fashioning him into the ideal of the gentle, softly spoken, post-modern advocate for love and individual rights and freedoms. But the fact is that the historical Jesus proclaimed God's coming judgement in a way that would give any modern fire-and-brimstone preacher a run for his money. I am not saying that fundamentalist Christianity reflects the Jesus of history any better than the liberal version does – both co-opt him for their own ends – but on the topic of divine punishment the fundamentalist has at least preserved a grain of truth about Jesus that the other has discarded.[1]

THE KINGDOM COME

Central to Jesus' vision was the 'kingdom of God', an expression that appears many times on his lips across a range of sources.[2] Indeed, the Gospel of Mark makes the theme the starting point of his preaching:

> *After John was put in prison, Jesus went into Galilee, proclaiming the good news of God. 'The time has*

> *come,' he said. 'The kingdom of God has come near. Repent and believe the good news!' (Mark 1:14–15; repeated in Matthew 4:17).*

The idea at the core of the Jewish hope for the kingdom was (and still is) the establishment of God's will on earth, proving him to be 'king'. It is the restoration of creation – social structures as well as the physical environment – to its rightful order. This theme is found in numerous Jewish texts from the period.[3] If you have ever found yourself wishing the Almighty (assuming he exists) would do something about the mess in the world, then you have, in a sense, hoped for what the Jews called the kingdom of God.

Because it entailed the righting of all wrongs, the kingdom was usually thought of as '*good* news', as Jesus says in the passage just quoted. Hence, Jesus taught his disciples to pray for the kingdom's arrival (in the famous Lord's Prayer or Our Father): 'Our Father in heaven, hallowed be your name, *your kingdom come*.' But, of course, there was a flipside. The kingdom of God would remove all that was contrary to the divine will, so its arrival necessarily entailed the display of God's judgement against evil. This is the context in which we are to think about Jesus' 'hell-fire' preaching.

THE HELL-FIRE PREACHER

The evidence that Jesus, like John the Baptist before him, warned his contemporaries of God's impending judgement is simply overwhelming. Professor Dale C. Allison – one of the leading Gospels scholars today *and no religious fundamentalist* – has compiled a list of no fewer than thirty-one passages (mostly from our earliest Gospel sources: Q, L, M and Mark) that capture Jesus speaking on this theme:[4]

- he pronounced 'woes' against the Pharisees and teachers of the law for their obsession with minutiae and neglect of compassion and justice;[5]

- he spoke of a great reversal of fortunes for the rich who oppress the poor;[6]
- he insisted that those who judged/condemned others would find themselves judged/condemned by God;[7]
- he warned of 'weeping and gnashing of teeth' for those who saw the kingdom of God as a birthright;[8]
- he prophesied that the Jerusalem Temple, the tangible sign of God's presence in the world, would be swiftly destroyed;[9]
- he even said that towns in his home district of Galilee, if they refused to heed his warning, would suffer a fate worse than that of proverbial 'Sodom'.[10]

It is quite a list.

I admit that the modern 'hell-fire preacher' is an odious cliché, and most of us today prefer the notion of an *approving* rather than a *judging* God. But none of this should blind us to what is really there in the historical record. Jesus saw something profoundly wrong in his people, especially amongst the leadership. In his view, they had replaced God's commands with their own; they had trampled on the poor and pandered to the rich; they had confused religion with social status; and, worst of all, they had refused to respond to his (and the Baptist's) call for urgent renewal. All that was left, then, was for the judge of the world to release his 'axe' and cut down every fruitless tree. The kingdom of God demanded it.

Many individuals of course *had* repented at the preaching of John. Many more would respond to the message of Jesus. But at the national level Jesus believed that Israel had become apostate. The chosen people had rejected their God. Now God was about to reject his people. This is a theme captured in one of his many so-called 'parables', in which he speaks of a 'vineyard' (a well-known image for Israel[11]) being handed to new owners:

> *'A man planted a vineyard. He put a wall around it, dug a pit for the winepress and built a watchtower. Then he rented the vineyard to some farmers and moved to another place. At harvest time he sent a servant to the tenants to collect from them some of the fruit of the vineyard. But they seized him, beat him and sent him away empty-handed. Then he sent another servant to them; they struck this man on the head and treated him shamefully. He sent still another, and that one they killed. He sent many others; some of them they beat, others they killed. He had one left to send, a son, whom he loved. He sent him last of all, saying, "They will respect my son." But the tenants said to one another, "This is the heir. Come, let's kill him, and the inheritance will be ours." So they took him and killed him, and threw him out of the vineyard. What then will the owner of the vineyard do? He will come and kill those tenants and give the vineyard to others' (Mark 12:1–9; repeated in Matthew 21:33–41 and Luke 20:9–16).*

Numerous other parables of Jesus focus on the theme of judgement against Israel (and the world).[12]

Later, we will see that Jesus' reputation as a herald of judgement was greatly moderated (the Pharisees thought *contradicted*) by his equally striking reputation as a 'friend of tax-collectors and sinners'.[13] The urgency of Jesus' warning of divine punishment was matched only by the intensity of his promise of divine forgiveness for those who 'repented', who decided to change. Love was never very far away from his proclamation of justice. Both had to do with the kingdom of God. The kingdom would remove what was contrary to God's will and establish what was in accordance with it. And the divine will could be summarized as *love*.

TWIN LOVES

No theme is more naturally associated with the figure of Jesus than that of 'love' (though after all this talk of judgement it may not seem so obvious). Here too he seems to have parted ways with many of the teachers of his day.

Jesus' teaching about love is widely regarded as one of the most historically secure pieces of information we have about him. The criterion of multiple attestation, in which numerous independent texts affirm a particular detail, is amply fulfilled here. An overwhelming number of sources make reference to the theme (Q, Mark, L, 1 John and others).[14]

Jesus summarized God's will with the double command to love God and love your neighbour. When challenged by one of the teachers of the law to name the most important commandment in God's law, Jesus replied that there are in fact *two* 'most important' commands and both come from the Old Testament itself:

> *One of the teachers of the law came and heard them debating. Noticing that Jesus had given them a good answer, he asked him, 'Of all the commandments, which is the most important?'*
>
> *'The most important one,' answered Jesus, 'is this: "Hear, O Israel: The Lord our God, the Lord is one. Love the Lord your God with all your heart and with all your soul and with all your mind and with all your strength" [Deuteronomy 6:5]. The second is this: "Love your neighbour as yourself" [Leviticus 19:18]. There is no commandment greater than these.'*
>
> *'Well said, teacher,' the man replied. 'You are right in saying that God is one and there is no other but him. To love him with all your heart, with all your understanding and with all your strength, and to love your neighbour as yourself is more important than all burnt offerings and sacrifices.' When Jesus*

> *saw that he had answered wisely, he said to him, 'You are not far from the kingdom of God.' And from then on no one dared ask him any more questions (Mark 12:28–34).*

Jesus' call for these 'twin loves' (of God and neighbour) left no room either for the neighbourly agnostic or for the spiritually minded hypocrite. The one may care for human beings but neglect the Creator; the other may be devoted to God but is careless towards the neighbour. Both are remiss in the mind of Jesus. Both have departed from the wishes of the Maker. Both deserve the coming judgement. In light of the modern aversion to any notion of 'sin' – usually defined in terms of the vices – we would do well to recall Jesus' own definition of what is required of human beings before the Almighty: love for the Creator and for our fellow creatures. *Falling short* of this goal (which is what the ancient word for 'sin' means) is what makes one a sinner. The curious upshot of Jesus' emphasis on the twin loves is that the 'religious' and the 'moral' can prove themselves sinners just as easily as the irreligious and the immoral.

LOVE OF ENEMIES

Jesus was not unique in stressing the importance of love in the spiritual life. As mentioned, shortly before him, Rabbi Hillel spoke of 'loving people and drawing them near to the Torah'.[15] Other Jewish writers also linked love of God with love of neighbours.[16] Love was a very Jewish theme. Having said that, Judaism's ethic of love seems to have found intense expression in the teaching of Jesus, particularly as it applies to those not normally considered 'neighbours'.

Jesus appears to have redefined who the recipients of neighbourly love ought to be. I recently had the honour of interviewing Geza Vermes, the Oxford Professor of Jewish

Studies. Amongst the many interesting things he said as we wandered through the beautiful grounds of The Oxford Centre for Hebrew and Jewish Studies was that 'neighbour' in the Old Testament command to 'Love your neighbour as yourself' is most naturally interpreted in the context of Leviticus 19 as a reference to the *Jewish* neighbour. He went on to point out that on the lips of Jesus the command took on a radical meaning – not utterly unique but striking in its intensity. Love was to be shown across racial and religious boundaries, even towards sinners and enemies.[17] Professor Vermes had in mind some particular statements from Q:

> *'Blessed are you who are poor, for yours is the kingdom of God. Blessed are you who hunger now, for you will be satisfied. Blessed are you who weep now, for you will laugh. Blessed are you when people hate you, when they exclude you and insult you and reject your name as evil…*
>
> *'But to you who are listening I say: Love your enemies, do good to those who hate you, bless those who curse you, pray for those who mistreat you. If someone slaps you on one cheek, turn the other also. If someone takes your coat, do not withhold your shirt. Give to everyone who asks you, and if anyone takes what belongs to you, do not demand it back. Do to others as you would have them do to you.*
>
> *'If you love those who love you, what credit is that to you? Even sinners love those who love them. And if you do good to those who are good to you, what credit is that to you? Even sinners do that. And if you lend to those from whom you expect repayment, what credit is that to you? Even sinners lend to sinners, expecting to be repaid in full. But love your enemies, do good to them, and*

> *lend to them without expecting to get anything back. Then your reward will be great, and you will be children of the Most High, because he is kind to the ungrateful and wicked. Be merciful, just as your Father is merciful' (Luke 6:20–36 | Matthew 5:3–11; 39–48).*

Other Jewish scholars likewise see Jesus as *intensifying* Judaism's already existent ethic of love. David Flusser, Professor of History of Religion at the Hebrew University of Jerusalem, has even described Jesus' command to love one's enemies as a kind of 'revolution'.[18] Certainly, it was revolutionary in the context of first-century Palestine, where for decades a very different sort of revolution had been brewing, one that wanted to throw off the shackles of Rome.

In 4 BC Judah son of Hezekiah led a rebellion in Sepphoris, near Jesus' hometown of Nazareth. The Romans responded swiftly and brutally.[19] Ten years later (AD 6) Judas the Galilean inspired many to fight against an increase in Roman taxation. Many were slaughtered.[20] When full-scale war with Rome broke out in AD 66 one of the key agitators was Menachem, the son of Judas the Galilean. Two more of his sons, James and Simon, were crucified by the Romans.[21] And another relative, Eleazar, led the defence of Masada, the heroic and gruesome last stand against the Romans in May AD 73.[22] Freedom fighting and hatred of the Romans ran deep in this Galilean family, as many in this period were convinced that the long-awaited kingdom of God would come through force.[23] The words 'love your enemies, do good to those who hate you' suggested more than just being nice to the annoying neighbour over the back fence. It implied showing compassion towards those who would crush you, and the Romans must have been partly in mind. In Jesus' view, the kingdom would come without human force, for its central value was love.

IN-GROUP MORALITY?

All of this makes quite astonishing the claim of the 'nouveau atheists' that Jesus never implied that love should be shown across racial or religious boundaries. Richard Dawkins, for instance, assures us that 'Jesus was a devotee of the same in-group morality – coupled with out-group hostility – that was taken for granted in the Old Testament.'[24] Out-group hostility? This will come as a great surprise to anyone who has read some scholarship on this topic or simply the Gospels themselves.

Much closer to the mark is the conclusion of Rodney Stark, Professor of the Social Sciences at Baylor University in the US, who professes no religious commitment. He regards this radicalized love-ethic to be the key to Christianity's success in the first three centuries:

> *Therefore, as I conclude this study, I find it necessary to confront what appears to me to be the ultimate factor in the rise of Christianity… The simple phrase 'For God so loved the world…' would have puzzled an educated pagan. And the notion that the gods care how we treat one another would have been dismissed as patently absurd… This was the moral climate in which Christianity taught that mercy is one of the primary virtues – that a merciful God requires humans to be merciful… This was revolutionary stuff. Indeed, it was the cultural basis for the revitalisation of the Roman world groaning under a host of miseries.*[25]

I offer this quotation without at all suggesting that Christians have always embodied such love in their long history. Here, I am simply offering the historical observation that the early Christians were powerfully affected by the love-ethic they learnt from Jesus.

Jesus' intensification of the Jewish call for love was striking and subversive. The objects of love included enemies, occupiers and outsiders. His vision of a loving God who extends mercy to all who repent was to find concrete expression in the lives of those who claimed to follow him. This *was* revolutionary, even if the revolution started small, like a mustard seed, slowly and quietly reaching full bloom.

6

STRANGE CIRCLE OF FRIENDS

Jesus' critique of Israel is seen not only in the revolutionary things that he taught but also, perhaps especially, in the kinds of students he deliberately sought.

Later sources blur the unusual make-up of Jesus' circle of friends. Josephus, for instance, writing towards the end of the first century says that he 'won over many Jews and many of the Greeks'.[1] The Talmud (an ancient Jewish legal commentary) speaks of Jesus' influence on the entire nation: 'he enticed and led Israel astray'.[2] These generalizing references mask one of the most curious features of our earliest sources. Jesus chose to teach (and it does seem it was a choice) three rather unexpected circles of disciples: a core group of unremarkables known as 'the twelve', some women, and many of the so-called 'sinners' of his day. Jesus was sending a message to Israel that his revolution, the 'kingdom of God' as he called it, involved a fundamental redefinition of who God's people are.

THE TWELVE

All the Gospels affirm that Jesus selected just twelve disciples to form the core of his circle:

> *Jesus went up on a mountainside and called to him those he wanted, and they came to him. He appointed twelve that they might be with him and that he might send them out to preach and to have authority to drive out demons. These are the twelve he*

> *appointed: Simon (to whom he gave the name Peter), James son of Zebedee and his brother John (to them he gave the name Boanerges, which means 'sons of thunder'), Andrew, Philip, Bartholomew, Matthew, Thomas, James son of Alphaeus, Thaddaeus, Simon the Zealot and Judas Iscariot, who betrayed him (Mark 3:13–19; repeated in Matthew 10:1–4 and Luke 6:12–16; see also John 6:70–71).*[3]

Why did Jesus appoint 'twelve' representatives? Why not eleven, thirteen or forty-three? The answer is found in the story of ancient Israel, the story Jesus grew up with.

The story of Israel begins with a man by the name of… *Israel.* According to the narrative of Genesis, the first book of the Jewish Scriptures (and the modern Bible), the patriarch Abraham turned away from the gods of his native Mesopotamia and embraced the one true God known as Yahweh. Abraham fathered Isaac; Isaac fathered Jacob; and then Jacob fathered twelve more sons. After a certain wrestling match with an angel, this Jacob came to be known as 'Israel', from the Hebrew word for 'struggle/strive'. His twelve sons then became the chiefs of what would be called the 'twelve tribes of Israel'. Henceforth, the number 'twelve' became a sign of the entirety of God's people.[4]

Centuries later Jesus chose *twelve* men to learn and to preach his message of renewal, of a new beginning, for Israel. Can this be an accident? Probably not. And in a passage from Q Jesus reveals to his twelve apostles the connection between them and the twelve tribes of Israel:

> *'Truly I tell you, at the renewal of all things, when the Son of Man sits on his glorious throne, you who have followed me will also sit on twelve thrones, judging the twelve tribes of Israel' (Matthew 19:28 | Luke 22:29–30).*

Just as Israel had begun with twelve tribes, so Jesus appointed twelve men who themselves were a sign and symbol of the 'renewal of all things' that Jesus was enacting. Some popular writers, notably Bishop Spong,[5] have thought that the number 'twelve' was a later invention of the Gospel writers, but virtually every scholar writing on Jesus today ranks this as one of the most secure facts of the story. Not only are the twelve referred to in Mark, Q, L, John and Paul[6] – all independent sources – devising symbols like this is exactly what we would expect from a prophet-like figure such as Jesus. 'Symbolic actions,' writes Professor Ed Sanders of Duke University, 'were part of a prophet's vocabulary. They simultaneously drew attention and conveyed information.'[7] Some of the greatest prophets of the Old Testament symbolized their message in vivid ways – marrying a harlot as a sign of God's devotion to adulterous Israel,[8] publicly eating bread cooked over human excrement as a picture of national defilement[9] and so on. By selecting twelve men as his representatives, Jesus was publicly symbolizing Israel's rebirth. As Professor Graham Stanton of the University of Cambridge puts it:

> *The importance of the call of the twelve can scarcely be exaggerated. In this prophetic action Jesus is calling for the renewal of Israel. He is also expressing the conviction that God is now beginning to establish anew his people – and will bring this to fulfilment.*[10]

The fact that Jesus himself was not part of the group – that it was not eleven + Jesus – suggests the even more daring claim that Jesus stood *apart from* and *over* this redefined people of God. Here, then, is a claim to maximum authority in Israel.[11] Jesus was, of course, a Jew, a son of the nation of Israel. At the same time, he obviously saw himself not as a *member* of Israel but as its Master.

THE WOMEN IN JESUS' LIFE

If Jesus' selection of 'the twelve' sent a provocative message to Israel about God's intention to redefine his people, then so did his invitation to women to join his circle.

But, first, a caveat. It is tempting to rush into a topic like this and portray Jesus as the archetypal feminist, a man before his time who sought to liberate women and overturn all forms of patriarchy. This is a sure-fire way to win female fans for Jesus (and for the author too). John Shelby Spong runs this line in a very animated chapter of *Jesus for the Non-Religious.* Jesus, we are told, broke down all boundaries and offered women a fullness of life rarely glimpsed in the history of the world (and the church). Spong says he taught them, included them and even elevated them to apostolic status. It is curious how very trusting the bishop suddenly becomes when the New Testament supports something he likes.[12]

But such modern, pro-women intuitions (mine as well as Spong's) cannot be allowed to run amuck with the historical evidence. Nor should we permit modern ecclesiastical debates about women's ordination to muddy the waters of a discussion about what was going on in the first century. Professor Paula Fredriksen of Boston University has sounded a potent caution to contemporary writers on Jesus. She urges us *not* to read our own ethical ideals and agenda into the story: 'the more facile the ethical or political relevance that a particular construct of Jesus presents,' she writes, 'the more suspect its worth as history. Only ancient evidence, not modern agendas, can reveal what might have mattered to ancient people.'[13] Feeling suitably admonished by this distinguished scholar (and woman), I want to unpack the 'ancient evidence' about the women in Jesus' life.

One of the little-known facts about Jesus' life is that it was women who bankrolled his mission. You have probably never stopped to wonder how much it might have cost to travel throughout Palestine – as a party of thirteen – over a two to three year period. Jesus and his disciples no doubt enjoyed generous hospitality in many of the towns and villages they visited, but this cannot have provided all of the food, lodging and taxes needed for the team. Even assuming Jesus and his disciples lived modestly – a fair assumption – the bill for his two to three year preaching tour would have been significant.[14] Where did the money come from? Tucked away in the Gospel of Luke is the probable answer:

> *After this, Jesus travelled about from one town and village to another, proclaiming the good news of the kingdom of God. The Twelve were with him, and also some women who had been cured of evil spirits and diseases: Mary (called Magdalene) from whom seven demons had come out; Joanna the wife of Chuza, the manager of Herod's household; Susanna; and many others. These women were helping to support them out of their own means (Luke 8:1–3).*

As Professor John Meier (University of Notre Dame) observes, this passage 'preserves a valuable historical memory… certain devoted women followers accompanied Jesus on his journeys around Galilee and finally up to Jerusalem and actually supported him and his entourage with their own money, food, or property.'[15] Such a passing and uncontrived detail, one that was also potentially off-putting for ancient male readers of Luke, has a strong claim to historical reality, as scholars typically observe.[16]

Unusually, these women are said to have actually *travelled* with Jesus. They were not like modern missionary supporters who send money, often by electronic transfer, from the comfort of their homes. These women joined Jesus (and the twelve) on tour throughout Galilee. The mere fact that Jesus invited women into such a visible role is unusual, to say the least, within a first-century Palestinian context.

Especially striking is the fact that these women followed Jesus all the way to Jerusalem and to his cross. All of the Gospels agree that whereas the leading male disciples fled after the arrest of Jesus, the women stayed as close as they could to him, watching from the back of the crowd as their beloved Master breathed his last:

> *Some women were watching from a distance. Among them were Mary Magdalene, Mary the mother of James the younger and of Joseph, and Salome. In Galilee these women had followed him and cared for his needs. Many other women who had come up with him to Jerusalem were also there (Mark 15:40–41; Luke 23:49; Matthew 27:55–56; John 19:25–27).*

The women remained faithful beyond the end. All four Gospels also indicate that after Jesus' death these women visited the tomb hoping to anoint his body with traditional burial spices. It was a final act of devotion even after the trauma of the crucifixion. And the devotion paid off. The texts are also unanimous that the women found the tomb empty and thus became the *first* witnesses to Jesus' resurrection.[17] Whatever we believe about the resurrection itself, the place of the women in the resurrection story is powerful historical testimony to the visibility of women in the life of Jesus and its aftermath. From the cradle to the grave (literally) women were prominent in the story of Jesus. In its ancient context this is striking. It would be anachronistic to paint Jesus as the harbinger of women's liberation, but there is no question that his vision of the kingdom of God had a conspicuous place for, and was surprisingly well received by, both halves of the human family.

THE 'SINNERS'

But just as remarkable as Jesus' selection of the twelve and his inclusion of women was his deeply scandalous practice of befriending and even dining with those classed as 'sinners'. The theme has always resonated with me ever since my high school Scripture teacher – one of Jesus' modern women – plucked up the courage to invite my classmates and me, none of whom was religious, for 'hamburgers, milkshakes and scones' and 'discussion about God'. We accepted the invitation, motivated in part by the free food, and filled this poor woman's sitting room with some of the most irreligious lads in the school – the bully, the drug-user, the thief and more. We had no idea at the time, as we returned week by week, that she was deliberately embodying one of the most striking and secure features of the life of the historical Jesus, what scholars call his 'table fellowship' with sinners.

Passages in Mark, Q and L all attest (independently) to a truly scandalous feature in Jesus' ministry. 'To his contemporaries,' writes Professor Ben F. Meyer of McMaster University in Canada in his celebrated *The Aims of Jesus*, 'it was a staggering phenomenon that he did not shrink from dining with the irreligious; indeed, he did so at his own initiative.'[18] The classic text is from Mark and is repeated in Matthew and Luke:

> *While Jesus was having dinner at Levi's house, many tax collectors and sinners were eating with him and his disciples, for there were many who followed him. When the teachers of the law who were Pharisees saw him eating with the sinners and tax collectors, they asked his disciples: 'Why does he eat with tax collectors and sinners?' On hearing this, Jesus said to them, 'It is not the healthy who need a doctor, but the sick. I have not come to call the righteous, but sinners' (Mark 2:15–17; repeated in Matthew 9:9–13 and Luke 5:27–32).*

There are debates about what exactly characterized the 'sinners'. Were they simply common folk whose vulgar trades and lack of education left them ignorant of the noble ways of Judaism and prone to moral lapses? Or were they the truly wicked, who systematically and flagrantly defied God's ways? The truth of the matter probably lies, as it so often does, somewhere in between. We can accept that 'sinners' were 'wicked' as long as we do not imagine that they were all murderers, drunkards or thieves. They could just as easily be 'ordinary' folk who neglected their religious duties or overlooked the poor. Either way, Jesus believed that they were 'sick' and that he had come as their 'doctor', offering them forgiveness and pointing them to the path of love (of God and neighbour).

The tag 'sinner' was potent. The clichéd sound of it today should not hide the fact that in the first century it was full of invective for those who used it. The *Psalms of Solomon,* a Jewish text (probably of Pharisaic persuasion) written in Jerusalem shortly before Jesus was born, declares:

> *But they [the righteous] shall pursue sinners and overtake them, for those who act lawlessly shall not escape the Lord's judgement. They shall be overtaken as by those experienced in war, for on their forehead is the mark of destruction. And the inheritance of sinners is destruction and darkness.*[19]

The seventeenth chapter of this document goes on to say how the hoped-for messiah would 'smash the arrogance of sinners like a potter's jar' and 'condemn sinners by the thoughts of their hearts'.[20] We can say with some confidence that there was nothing 'messianic' about Jesus' habit of dining with and befriending sinners.

In order to appreciate the scandal caused by Jesus' dining habits we have to picture a time when sitting down at a table with others was a powerful symbol of *fellowship* with them. Eating together was a statement: 'it indicated that the invited person was being accepted into a relationship in which the bonds were as close as in family relations,' says Professor Graham Stanton of the University of Cambridge. 'One normally invited to meals only people whom one considered social and religious equals.'[21] Hence, by Jesus' day Jewish teachers had laid down strict rules about who could be your dining companion.[22]

For many in Jesus' time, impurity was 'contagious'. Contact with sinners therefore had the potential to make even the righteous unclean and so unable to commune with God. Within such a setting it becomes easy to understand the shock that Jesus caused by gladly welcoming those normally considered out of bounds. The shock turned into insult. A passage from Q records what the establishment were saying about Jesus: 'Here is a glutton and a drunkard, a friend of tax collectors and sinners.'[23] Many religious folk today may puzzle at how Jesus could have invited such slander, but most experts regard this scandal over Jesus' dining habits as one of the most secure pieces of our evidence about him.

Why did Jesus eat with the immoral and irreligious? Why did he leave himself open to the charge of being a 'glutton and a drunkard' and the 'friend of sinners'? The first thing to say is that Jesus was not approving of the behaviour of the sinners. It is quite clear that he called *everyone* to the life of radical renewal defined by his teaching. All were to love God with all their heart and their neighbour as themselves. Sinners, by definition, were not fulfilling this twofold imperative. Jesus did not confine his warnings of judgement to the spiritual elite. A passage from Q makes plain that even the ordinary folk living in the towns and villages of Galilee were destined, if they failed to heed Jesus' call, to be condemned when God's kingdom is revealed in the world:

> *'Woe to you, Chorazin! Woe to you, Bethsaida! If the miracles that were performed in you had been*

> *performed in Tyre and Sidon, they would have repented long ago in sackcloth and ashes. But I tell you, it will be more bearable for Tyre and Sidon on the day of judgement than for you. And you, Capernaum, will you be lifted up to the skies? No, you will go down to the depths. If the miracles that were performed in you had been performed in Sodom, it would have remained to this day. But I tell you that it will be more bearable for Sodom on the day of judgement than for you' (Matthew 11:21–24 | Luke 10:12–15).*

If Jesus proclaimed the coming judgement, then why on earth did he fraternize with those soon to be condemned? This was the question of the religious leaders. The answer accepted by most scholars today is that Jesus' open table fellowship was another deliberate sign of his message of renewal for Israel (similar to his selection of the twelve). By deliberately seeking opportunities to dine with sinners Jesus was embodying the friendship with sinners that he believed God wanted to achieve. There was a message of love here, but it was not a love that left the beloved unchanged. It was a transformative love. Jesus apparently thought that purity – *his* purity – was a more powerful contagion (if that is the right word) than sin. When Jesus invited sinners to dine with him, he was confident that the welcoming grace of God would overwhelm, and therefore transform, those who ate at his table. He believed in a kind of 'contagious holiness' – which is the title of a major book on this subject.[24]

According to Jesus, God was about to act in a decisive way to renew and redefine Israel. What he called 'the kingdom of God' was soon to appear and nothing would be the same again. This new Israel – symbolized by the selection of the twelve – not only affirmed women as full participants and patrons of the movement, it also called sinners into its fellowship, inviting them to the banquet of God's transforming love.

7

MIRACLES, HISTORY AND THE KINGDOM

The historian faces a real dilemma in the study of Jesus. Everything appears to be going along just fine. The sources are analysed, the methods applied, the background assessed and, slowly but surely, a plausible picture of the man from Nazareth begins to emerge. Then suddenly we are confronted by an aspect of the story that threatens to call the whole enterprise into question. The 'miracles' of Jesus, his healings, exorcisms and mastery over nature, leave us wondering whether we have been using the historical method to study a fairytale. Consider the following, fairly representative, passage from the Gospel of Mark:

> *They went to Capernaum, and when the Sabbath came, Jesus went into the synagogue and began to teach. The people were amazed at his teaching, because he taught them as one who had authority, not as the teachers of the law. Just then a man in their synagogue who was possessed by an evil spirit cried out, 'What do you want with us, Jesus of Nazareth? Have you come to destroy us? I know who you are – the Holy One of God!' 'Be quiet!' said Jesus sternly. 'Come out of him!' The evil spirit shook the man violently and came out of him with a shriek. The people were all so amazed that they asked each other, 'What is this? A new teaching – and with authority! He even gives orders to evil spirits and*

> *they obey him.' News about him spread quickly over the whole region of Galilee.*
>
> *As soon as they left the synagogue, they went with James and John to the home of Simon and Andrew. Simon's mother-in-law was in bed with a fever, and they immediately told Jesus about her. So he went to her, took her hand and helped her up. The fever left her and she began to wait on them.*
>
> *That evening after sunset the people brought to Jesus all the sick and demon-possessed. The whole town gathered at the door, and Jesus healed many who had various diseases. He also drove out many demons, but he would not let the demons speak because they knew who he was (Mark 1:21–34).*

In a contemporary context, stories like these seem to many to be the stuff of ancient legend, not the reporting of historical events. And so the historian puzzles over what this might mean for the entire Gospel narrative. Just about every serious volume on Jesus begins its discussion of the 'miracles' with a preamble, sometimes quite lengthy, admitting the dilemma and explaining why it is necessary to push through and explore the topic: we know it defies modern sensibilities, they say, but it is there in the sources and we have to deal with it.[1]

HOW HISTORIANS 'COPE' WITH THE MIRACLES OF JESUS

The problem would evaporate if healing stories were marginal to the Jesus story or if they were found only in a single, late source (for example, if they only appeared in the Gospel of John). Then scholars could dismiss the stories as tangential, accretions to an evolving legend. But things are not so simple. Stories and/or sayings about Jesus' healings and exorcisms are found across a surprising range of sources: in Mark, Q, L, M and the source behind John's Gospel known as SQ. Even the first-century Jewish writer, Josephus, describes Jesus as 'one who wrought surprising feats'.[2] The expression 'surprising feats' translates the Greek *paradoxa erga*, literally 'baffling deeds'. It is the Jewish historian's hesitant, non-committal way of relating Jesus' widespread fame as a miracle-worker.

In other words, the best sources and methods employed by the leading scholars in the field produce the unexpected – and for some *embarrassing* – conclusion that the *paradoxa erga* of Jesus are, as Professor James Dunn (Durham University) admits, 'one of the most widely attested and firmly established of the historical facts with which we have to deal'.[3]

So, how do historians 'cope' with the unpalatable conclusion that Jesus was known as a successful healer and exorcist? One thing is clear: they do not retreat from history in the way Bishop John Shelby Spong does in his *Jesus for the Non-Religious.* For Spong, reports of miracles cannot be historical. They must therefore be metaphorical:

> *I hope it is now obvious that in each of these so-called miraculous accounts of Jesus giving sight to the blind, the stories are designed not to relate a supernatural event, but to focus the ongoing debate on the identity of Jesus. By reading them literally, we have in effect blinded countless generations of Christians from understanding the real meaning of these stories. Signs of the in-breaking kingdom of God are attached to the life of Jesus, who was said to embody that kingdom by opening the eyes of those who are blind so that they might see their deepest identity.*[4]

Far from reading the sources as metaphorical at this point, however, contemporary scholars universally agree that Jesus was known in his day as a healer. Objective analysis of the historical record can lead to no other conclusion. Resorting to a symbolic interpretation of the data involves special pleading. Even scholars who reject the possibility of the supernatural, such as Boston University's Professor Paula Fredriksen and DePaul University's Professor John Dominic Crossan, still affirm that *Jesus did things that were widely interpreted from the beginning as miracles.*[5] In other words, his reputation at the time as a healer and exorcist may be regarded as beyond reasonable doubt. This is a conclusion reached by virtually everyone writing in the field today, making it one of the most striking and stable points of consensus in Jesus scholarship over the last three decades. A glance at any of the serious books on Jesus listed in the bibliography will reveal how thorough is Bishop Spong's disengagement from the mainstream scholarly conversation about Jesus' miracles.[6]

THE MEANING OF THE MIRACLES

What meaning was attached to Jesus' healings and exorcisms and, in particular, what meaning did *Jesus* attach to them? We can answer this historical question with a surprising degree of confidence. We have at least two statements about the miracles from Jesus' own lips, and both are found in our earliest Gospel source, Q, written down in the 50s AD.

There was a dispute in Galilee over the source of Jesus' power to drive out demons. Some in the crowd attributed this ability to a chief demonic entity known as Beelzebul (the origin of the word is completely obscure). Jesus offers another interpretation:

> *Jesus was driving out a demon that was mute. When the demon left, the man who had been mute spoke, and the crowd was amazed. But some of them said, 'By Beelzebul, the prince of demons, he is driving out demons.' Others tested him by asking for a sign from heaven. Jesus knew their thoughts and said to them:*

> *'Any kingdom divided against itself will be ruined, and a house divided against itself will fall. If Satan is divided against himself, how can his kingdom stand? I say this because you claim that I drive out demons by Beelzebul. Now if I drive out demons by Beelzebul, by whom do your followers drive them out? So then, they will be your judges. But if I drive out demons by the finger of God, then the kingdom of God has come upon you' (Luke 11:14–20 | Matthew 12:22–28).*[7]

That Jesus was accused by some – no doubt the leadership – of being in league with the devil may be regarded as certain. Not only is a very similar accusation found independently in the Gospels of Mark and John,[8] but it makes no sense at all that Christians would invent such a charge, potentially sowing seeds of doubt into the minds of readers. A later Jewish text continues this negative interpretation of Jesus' powers. Tractate *Sanhedrin* of the Talmud justifies his execution on the grounds that 'he practised sorcery and led Israel astray'.[9] 'Sorcery' in Jewish law was punishable by death because, unlike mere trickery, it was thought to involve dark powers.

But more important than the historicity of the charge is Jesus' striking defence and, in particular, his own interpretation of his baffling deeds: 'if I drive out demons by the finger of God, then the kingdom of God has come upon you'. Far from being displays of dark energy, Jesus' deeds were evidence that God's long-awaited rule over the world had begun to dawn. We have already seen that the 'kingdom of God' was a central theme of his preaching. Here we discover that it also provided the lens through which he understood his ministry of healing.

According to Jewish tradition, one day God would establish his kingdom in the world, overthrowing evil and restoring human life to its intended state. The whole creation, including its social realities, would be renewed. Exorcism and healing were vivid pictures of these realities. Jesus was signalling that the *future* kingdom was somehow present *right now*. The era Jews longed for, when God would put an end to suffering and renew creation to its full glory, could be glimpsed, or previewed, in events taking place in Galilee between AD 28 and 30. His healing ministry constituted a profound theological statement to Israel – similar to his selection of the twelve and his eating with sinners. God's promise to renew his people (and the world) was being actualized in the baffling deeds of the teacher from Nazareth. This was without precedent in antiquity, as Professors Gerd Theissen and Annette Merz of the University of Heidelberg note:

> *Nowhere else do we find a charismatic miracle worker whose miraculous deeds are meant to be the end of an old world and the beginning of a new one. This puts a tremendous emphasis on the miracles (and it is unhistorical to relativize their significance for the historical Jesus). The present thus becomes a time of salvation in microcosm.*[10]

There is also an unmistakable claim to authority inherent in Jesus' own understanding of his baffling deeds. In his activity the kingdom of God was being revealed, he claimed. As with his selection of the twelve to symbolize God's new people (over which he stood as Master), Jesus here presents himself as the locus of the divine renewal.

MIRACLES AND BELIEF

Imagine for a moment that this chapter had not been about healings and exorcisms but about some *earthly* aspect of Jesus' ministry that enjoyed the same degree of historical support. Let's say, for instance, that we had been exploring the unparalleled (and fictitious) habit of Jesus breaking into song in the middle of his teachings. Suppose this practice were mentioned in all four Gospels and in all of the Gospel sources (Q, L, etc.) and that the non-Christian writer Josephus also made mention of Jesus' *paradoxa humnoi*, 'baffling songs'. What would we make of it? We would surely accept it; the historical evidence would demand it.

Needless to say, I am not offering this as an argument in favour of Jesus' healings. I am simply highlighting that the modern reticence to accept the Gospels' claims about this matter has little to do with history and much to do with our views about the universe. Philosophically, the rationality (or otherwise) of acknowledging the possibility of miracles boils down to our prior assumptions about the world. If we assume that the laws of nature are the only things regulating the universe, then we will feel justified in rejecting all claims of miracles *in principle*. No amount of historical evidence will be considered good enough to convince us that a miracle has taken place.

This is a position championed with characteristic gusto by Richard Dawkins in Chapter 3 of *The God Delusion*. There he discusses the report that 70,000 pilgrims at Fatima in Portugal in 1917 saw the sun 'tear itself from the heavens and come crashing down upon the multitude'.[11] He admits that such widely offered testimony is 'harder to write off' than other miracle stories, but he promptly insists that *any* naturalistic explanation is preferable to the supernatural one. Perhaps it was a mass hallucination, Dawkins muses, or perhaps a giant fraud: 'any of these apparent improbabilities is far more probable than the alternative: that the Earth was suddenly yanked sideways in its orbit, and the solar system destroyed, with nobody outside Fatima noticing'.

Dawkins is, of course, hamming things up for effect. He must know that what the pilgrims claimed to have seen was a *vision*, not an astronomical cataclysm: none of them reported injuries after experiencing the sun fall in on them. But there is a more important point. Dawkins is fudging a little with his philosophy (the way a lecturer might fudge when delivering material for the first time: talk quickly and leave no time for questions). He never explains *why* a natural explanation must trump a supernatural one every time. Presumably, it is just self-evident to him. He holds that there is no God and that the laws of nature are the only things regulating the universe; therefore, miracles can never be established by evidence. Though unacknowledged, his atheism is the *premise* of his argument at this point, not its logical deduction.[12]

To reiterate: the dogmatic rejection of miracles has little to do with evidence and a lot to do with existing assumptions about what is possible in the universe. The person who believes that the observable laws of nature are the *only things* regulating the universe will, as I said, feel well justified in following Dawkins and others in denying miracles. Conversely, the person who believes that there is a law-giver behind the laws of nature will feel justified in remaining open to the possibility of miracles, even while remaining generally sceptical about any particular miraculous claim. But we must all acknowledge that in both cases it is our assumption, not evidence, that influences the conclusion. As Professor John Meier of the University of Notre Dame remarks:

> *The atheist's judgement may be as firm and sincere as the believer's; it is also just as much a philosophical or theological judgement, determined by a particular worldview, and not a judgement that arises simply, solely, and necessarily out of an examination of the evidence of this particular case.*[13]

The historical material about Jesus' baffling deeds is impressive. The stalemate occurs at the philosophical level, at the level of our prior assumptions. This is not the book for that discussion.

8

CONTRA JERUSALEM

Arriving in Jerusalem for the first time is a very strange experience. One of the first things visitors do is drive to the top of the so-called Mount of Olives 1 kilometre (0.6 miles) east of the city and take in the spectacular view of this iconic place. It is very beautiful. Directly below you on the mountain slope is the famous Jewish cemetery facing the Temple Mount, ready for the day of resurrection. It is a reminder of the spiritual meaning of this spot. Immediately in front, where the Jewish Temple once stood, is the enormous golden Dome of the Rock and the Al-Aqsa Mosque, one of the three most holy sites in Islam. An amazing combination of very modern and truly ancient buildings dots the landscape as you try to take in the fact that Jerusalem has been continually inhabited for almost 6,000 years.

For me, standing on the Mount of Olives overlooking Jerusalem was a surreal experience more than a spiritual one. For ancient Jews, however, the religious significance of this place is impossible to exaggerate.

THE MEANING OF JERUSALEM

According to the Jewish Scriptures, the city was first captured for the Israelites by King David a millennium before Jesus. It was his administrative capital for the remaining thirty years of his reign.[1] Significantly, his son Solomon built a Temple for the Lord in Jerusalem and from that time on, the Temple Mount – and by extension, the city itself – was believed to be the dwelling place of God on earth. Israel's Lord ruled the entire universe, of course, but he condescended to touch the world at just this point. As a result, the Jewish feeling about this city is not just cultural and historical but profoundly theological.

Reinforcing this outlook is the fact that Jews were required to make pilgrimage to Jerusalem on three occasions each year: the Feast of Tabernacles (Sukkot), which recalled Israel's nomadic wanderings in the desert; Passover (Pessah), the celebration of deliverance from Egypt; and the Feast of Weeks (Shavuot), a memorial of Moses' receiving of the law at Sinai. Of these, the Passover festival was by far the most popular. Jews throughout the Mediterranean would flock to Jerusalem, quadrupling the population of the city for the two-week celebrations in and around the Temple.[2]

Jews thought of these pilgrimages not as mere memorials but as opportunities to 'appear before the Lord'.[3] Going to the Jerusalem Temple meant going to God. The Temple of Jesus' day is gone – destroyed by the Romans in AD 70 – but the feeling of Jews towards the city and the Temple Mount is unchanged. I found this out recently when visiting the famous Wailing Wall, the western edge of the ancient Temple precinct. I was struck by the enormous 'tourist information' plaque near the entrance, which explains in Hebrew and English the history and significance of the place:

> *Jewish tradition teaches that the Temple Mount is the focal point of Creation. In the center of the mountain lies the 'Foundation Stone' of the world. Here Adam came into being. Here Abraham, Isaac and Jacob served God. The First and Second Temples were built upon this mountain. The Ark of the Covenant was set upon the Foundation Stone itself. Jerusalem was chosen by God as the dwelling place of the Shechinah [divine glory]. David longed to build the Temple, and Solomon his son built the First Temple here about*

> *3000 years ago. It was destroyed by Nevuchadnezzar of Babylon. The Second Temple was rebuilt on its ruins seventy years later. It was razed by the Roman legions over 1900 years ago. The present Western Wall before you is a remnant of the western Temple Mount retaining walls. Jews have prayed in its shadow for hundreds of years, an expression of their faith in the rebuilding of the Temple. The Sages said about it: 'The Divine Presence never moves from the Western Wall.' The Temple Mount continues to be the focus of prayer for Jews from all over the world.*

It was into this most holy city (and its Temple) that the teacher and healer from Galilee entered during the Passover festival of AD 30. He would be dead in a matter of days.

THE DONKEY AND THE CITY

Jesus' ministry was based up north in Galilee, but there came a time when his message of Israel's judgement and renewal had to be taken to the capital. According to all four Gospels, in the final weeks of Jesus' ministry he and his group of twelve (the sign of a new Israel) headed for Jerusalem to teach and heal and confront the historic power base of the nation.

Jesus' entry into Jerusalem is described in each of the Gospels. He came to the holy city from the east, over the top of the Mount of Olives and down into the city gates. As he did this he acted out – deliberately it seems – a famous Jewish prophecy about the arrival of God's appointed king. The ancient prophet Zechariah had foretold: 'Shout, Daughter of Jerusalem! See, your king comes to you, righteous and having salvation, gentle and riding on a donkey.'[4] With this in mind, surrounded by crowds of pilgrims making their way to the Passover festival, Jesus arranges his symbolically charged entrance:

> *As they approached Jerusalem and came to Bethphage and Bethany at the Mount of Olives, Jesus sent two of his disciples, saying to them, 'Go to the village ahead of you, and just as you enter it, you will find a colt tied there, which no one has ever ridden. Untie it and bring it here. If anyone asks you, "Why are you doing this?" say, "The Lord needs it and will send it back here shortly."' They went and found a colt outside in the street, tied at a doorway. As they untied it, some people standing there asked, 'What are you doing, untying that colt?' They answered as Jesus had told them to, and the people let them go. When they brought the colt to Jesus and threw their cloaks over it, he sat on it. Many people spread their cloaks on the road, while others spread branches they had cut in the fields. Those who went ahead and those who followed shouted, 'Hosanna! Blessed is he who comes in the name of the Lord! Blessed is the coming kingdom of our father David! Hosanna in the highest heaven!' Jesus entered Jerusalem and went into the temple courts (Mark 11:1–11; repeated in Matthew 21:1–9 and Luke 19:28–40; independently in John 12:12–19).*

Some scholars have doubted that this is an authentic scene from Jesus' life. It looks to them like a story crafted by the Gospel writers to make Jesus *appear* as the fulfilment of the prophecy of Zechariah. Most, however, accept it. Even typically sceptical scholars such as Professor Ed Sanders of Duke University and Professor Marcus Borg of Oregon State University acknowledge that the scene fits well with Jesus' penchant for prophet-like signs (such as the selection of the twelve and his dining with sinners). They conclude that this probably was a real event in his life.[5] The fact that the same story (with small variations) appears *independently* in the Gospel of John strengthens this conclusion.

Scholars continue to debate the meaning of Jesus' 'planned political demonstration', as Borg describes it.[6] Was it a claim to messianic status? Was it a statement about the kingdom of peace predicted in the Zechariah prophecy? The answer is: probably both. Here, for the first time, Jesus publicly casts himself – albeit in a symbolic action rather than an explicit statement – as the king over Israel, the messiah. Professor Ed Sanders, who tends to avoid saying that Jesus made messianic claims about himself, writes of this incident, 'I incline to the view that it was Jesus himself who read the prophecy and decided to fulfil it: that here he implicitly declared himself to be "king".'[7] God was about to disclose something of his kingdom in the holy city – this is the meaning of the incident – and the man on the donkey was central to it.

ACTION AGAINST THE TEMPLE

The next 'enacted parable', as Professor James Dunn (Durham University) calls it, brings some clarity to Jesus' intentions towards Jerusalem and its Temple. Upon entering Jerusalem Jesus marches into the sacred precinct and creates a dazzling disturbance. The incident is regarded as historically certain by most scholars and appears in all four Gospels:

> *On reaching Jerusalem, Jesus entered the temple courts and began driving out those who were buying and selling there. He overturned the tables of the money changers and the benches of those selling doves, and would not allow anyone to carry merchandise through the temple courts. And as he taught them, he said, 'Is it not written: "My house will be called a house of prayer for all nations"? But you have made it "a den of robbers".' The chief priests and the teachers of the law heard this and began looking for a way*

> *to kill him, for they feared him, because the whole crowd was amazed at his teaching (Mark 11:15–18; repeated in Matthew 21:12–17 and Luke 19:45–48; independently in John 2:13–17).*

Just so you are picturing all this on the correct scale, keep in mind that the Temple precinct was 300 metres (328 yards) long on its east–west axis and 500 metres (547 yards) wide on its north–south axis: twelve football fields, with stands, would fit into its area.[8]

You might be wondering why there were people 'buying and selling' in the Temple courts. This was a religious service controlled by the priests. At Passover time families were required to make various animal sacrifices. Rather than bring your lamb or doves from home, for convenience you could purchase them near the great southern square of the holy precinct known as the Court of the Gentiles. Once you collected your animal you proceeded to the Court of the Israelites (open only to Jewish males) and handed it over to a priest, who sacrificed it on your behalf. Obviously, the system could easily be abused by unscrupulous priests, since the officials could charge whatever price they determined.

Jesus apparently saw all this as an expression of worldly defilement amongst the Temple elite. Being a priest did not necessarily make you rich, but many in Jesus' day noted that the aristocracy was made up of a disproportionate number of priests. Jesus was not the first person to criticize such things: other Jewish texts written shortly before the time of Jesus refer to the priestly elite as defrauders and thieves.[9] But he certainly ramped up the criticism in a dramatic and confronting way.

Traditionally, this episode is known as the Cleansing of the Temple, and it has been the subject of numerous works of classical art.[10] The name suggests that Jesus intended to purge or reform the Temple service, making it more pleasing to God. But most scholars see it as a deliberate sign of the Temple's impending *destruction* by some grand intervention of God. Judgement on Israel is certainly a theme found frequently on Jesus' lips, and in some of his explicit sayings the Temple is said to be under threat. For example, in John's version of the Temple 'cleansing' we read:

> *The Jews then responded to him, 'What sign can you show us to prove your authority to do all this?' Jesus answered them, 'Destroy this temple, and I will raise it again in three days.' They replied, 'It has taken forty-six years to build this temple, and you are going to raise it in three days?' But the temple he had spoken of was his body (John 2:18–21).*[11]

Jesus' actions in the Temple were the climax of his proclamation of judgement. In Galilee, as we have seen, he accused his hearers of being obsessed with minutiae while neglecting the path of justice and compassion.[12] That such words were not directed only at religious leaders is clear from his denunciation of certain Galilean villages for their unwillingness to repent at his preaching.[13] It is this message of judgement – for leaders and lay – that Jesus took to the Temple, the heart of the nation's religious life.

It should be clear that Jesus is not personally threatening the Temple, as if he had some clandestine military plan up his sleeve. He is speaking of an apocalyptic event, a disclosure of God's own power.[14] As Professor Sean Freyne of Trinity College Dublin has demonstrated, Jesus rejected all attempts to realize God's kingdom through violence; he opted instead for the path of love and service, leaving the future of the kingdom entirely in God's hands.[15] *He* would not do anything to the Temple (apart from his prophetic sign); it would be God who would destroy it and miraculously establish it anew (in his own person, according to the passage above). This is an extraordinary thing to suggest in Jerusalem at Passover time. It is no wonder he would soon be dead.

THE DESTRUCTION OF THE TEMPLE IN AD 70

Within a generation of Jesus' symbolic action of overturning the priestly tables in the Temple, Palestine was embroiled in an un-winnable war with Rome, as Jews *en masse* sought to reclaim the holy land from their pagan overlords. In August AD 70, after five years of fierce fighting, Jerusalem found itself surrounded by the four legions of Titus (more than 20,000 men). They soon breached the walls and made their way to the Temple – a structure with a circumference of over 1.5 kilometres (1 mile). Josephus, who was an eyewitness to much of the war, describes the final bloody moments: 'The roar of the flames streaming far and wide mingled with the groans of the falling victims; and, owing to the height of the hill and the mass of the burning pile, one would have thought that the whole city was ablaze.'[16]

I am not saying that Jesus made a 'supernatural prophecy' that was divinely fulfilled a generation later. I am simply laying out the clear historical evidence that Jesus warned (through word and action) that the precious Jerusalem Temple would soon be destroyed. And it was. Whether one interprets this as a lucky guess on the part of Jesus or a sage piece of political foresight or a divinely inspired prophecy is not a historical matter, so it is not part of my argument.

I will say this. I recently found myself standing amid the massive rubble of the southern end of the Temple's western wall, and it truly was an eerie experience. I don't know if it was the Christian in me or just the historian, but as I stood there touching these enormous, charred monuments to Roman brutality and Jewish resistance I could not help imagining Jesus on this spot – or very near it, anyway – overturning tables, calling on Israel to repent and warning of a future catastrophe.

But, first, Jesus would face his own catastrophe, and his actions and words against the Temple were probably partly to blame.

9

LAST SUPPER

While a few scholars over the years have supposed that Jesus' arrest and execution took him completely by surprise, the vast majority believe that he must have had more than an inkling of where his controversial ministry was heading.[1] Jesus knew full well that some of Israel's most famous prophets had been killed by God's people,[2] and in several passages from the Gospel source known as Q he makes a point of mentioning it:

> *'Woe to you, because you build tombs for the prophets, and it was your ancestors who killed them. So you testify that you approve of what your ancestors did; they killed the prophets, and you build their tombs. Because of this, God in his wisdom said, "I will send them prophets and apostles, some of whom they will kill and others they will persecute." Therefore this generation will be held responsible for the blood of all the prophets that has been shed since the beginning of the world, from the blood of Abel to the blood of Zechariah, who was killed between the altar and the sanctuary. Yes, I tell you, this generation will be held responsible for it all' (Luke 11:47–51 | Matthew 23:29–35).*[3]

Given that his own ministry was so obviously based on the prophetic model, he must have thought it a real possibility that he too would be martyred, especially since his own mentor, John the Baptist, had suffered this fate just a year or two earlier.

Following his dramatic symbolic action in the Temple Jesus would have known that the tension between him and Israel's leaders was about to reach crisis point. It was Passover time. Religious feelings were running hot. He chose this moment to make clear to his disciples what was about to happen. The Passover meal itself became Jesus' famous Last Supper. The passage from Mark below is repeated in Matthew and appears independently in Luke and in one of the letters of Paul. Its historicity cannot be doubted. Even Professor Ed Sanders of Duke University admits, 'The passage has the strongest possible support':[4]

> *While they were eating [the Passover meal], Jesus took bread, and when he had given thanks, he broke it and gave it to his disciples, saying, 'Take it; this is my body.' Then he took the cup, and when he had given thanks, he gave it to them, and they all drank from it. 'This is my blood of the covenant, which is poured out for many,' he said to them (Mark 14:22–24; repeated in Matthew 26:26–29; independently in Luke 22:19–20 and 1 Corinthians 11:23–25).*

More impressive than the simple historical pedigree of the Last Supper account is the clear window it gives us into the thoughts of Jesus himself during the Passover festival of AD 30. It is worth pausing here and practising what scholars call a 'thought experiment', casting yourself imaginatively back into the historical situation described in the text. We have in these few words a poignant glimpse into the dying sentiments of one of the world's most influential men on the eve of one of history's most significant events. (Even those without any religious feeling must admit that the crucifixion of Jesus has had an incalculable impact on Western history.)

A NEW PASSOVER SACRIFICE

The first thing to observe is that Jesus' final meal took place during the great Passover festival, when tens of thousands of Jews flocked to Jerusalem to celebrate Israel's deliverance from Egypt centuries earlier. According to the biblical narrative recorded in the book of Exodus, centuries before Christ God's people were a slave nation under the control of the great superpower of the day. God's judgement fell upon the despotic pharaoh and his subjects but 'passed over' the children of Israel, so that they could escape Egypt and journey to the Promised Land. Central to the original event was the killing and eating of a lamb. The blood of the animal was to be sprinkled on the doorposts of Jewish households as a sign that, on account of the slain lamb, God's people were to be redeemed and not condemned. The account from the book of Exodus reads:

> *The Lord said to Moses and Aaron in Egypt, 'This month is to be for you the first month, the first month of your year. Tell the whole community of Israel that on the tenth day of this month each man is to take a lamb for his family, one for each household. If any household is too small for a whole lamb, they must share one with their nearest neighbour, having taken into account the number of people there are. You are to determine the amount of lamb needed in accordance with what each person will eat. The animals you choose must be year-old males without defect, and you may take them from the sheep or the goats. Take care of them until the fourteenth day of the month, when all the people of the community of Israel must slaughter them at twilight. Then they are to take some of the blood and put it on the sides and tops of the doorframes of the houses where they eat the lambs. That same*

> *night they are to eat the meat roasted over the fire, along with bitter herbs, and bread made without yeast. Do not eat the meat raw or cooked in water, but roast it over the fire – head, legs and inner parts. Do not leave any of it till morning; if some is left till morning, you must burn it. This is how you are to eat it: with your cloak tucked into your belt, your sandals on your feet and your staff in your hand. Eat it in haste; it is the Lord's Passover.*
>
> *'On that same night I will pass through Egypt and strike down every firstborn – both men and animals – and I will bring judgement on all the gods of Egypt. I am the Lord. The blood will be a sign for you on the houses where you are; and when I see the blood, I will pass over you. No destructive plague will touch you when I strike Egypt. This is a day you are to commemorate; for the generations to come you shall celebrate it as a festival to the Lord – a lasting ordinance' (Exodus 12:1–14).*

In Jesus' day the male representative of the household brought a lamb (or kid) to the Jerusalem Temple on the afternoon of the fourteenth of the month of Nisan. After presenting it to one of the thousands of priests on duty that day, the worshipper killed the animal while the priest caught the blood in a sacred bowl that he passed back along the priestly line to be tossed against the base of the Temple altar. The Passover lamb, then, was far more than a simple memorial; it had a clear *sacrificial* dimension. Its blood was literally poured out before the Lord and its fatty portions offered to him in sacrifice.[5]

This sacrificial dimension becomes important as we try to understand Jesus' striking words spoken during his farewell meal: 'This is my blood of the covenant, which is poured out for many.' There can be no doubt that he was speaking of his impending death in language intended to recall the lamb sacrificed for the deliverance of God's people. The blood of the original Passover lamb ensured that while judgement fell on Egypt it would 'pass over' Jewish households. In light of Jesus' consistent teaching about the judgement soon to fall on Israel (see Chapter 5), it is clear that he understood his sacrifice as the means by which people might escape the coming disaster.

THE MODERN AVERSION TO BLOOD

The idea of blood sacrifice for atonement, which so obviously stands behind the words of Jesus at the Last Supper, is often criticized today as barbaric and bloodthirsty. Richard Dawkins with typical zest describes it as 'vicious, sado-masochistic and repellent'. He also calls it 'barking mad' and asks, 'If God wanted to forgive our sins, why not just forgive them?'[6] The answer of the ancient Jew (and Christian) is that God must be (and appear to be) *just* in the performance of his mercy. As a judge may not freely release a convicted criminal simply because he is positively inclined towards him, so God does not forgive the guilty without exacting payment at the same time. That is the ancient logic of atonement, whether or not we like it. The unsurpassed historical study of this theme, entitled simply *The Atonement*, was written more than twenty-five years ago by the Professor of New Testament and Early Judaism at the University of Tübingen, Martin Hengel.[7]

At the centre of the Jewish legal code lay sacrificial atonement. The Old Testament book of Leviticus, for instance, describes the great Yom Kippur, or Day of Atonement, in which Israel's sins were symbolically transferred to a goat:

> *He [the high priest] shall then slaughter the goat for the sin offering for the people and take its blood behind the curtain and do with it as he did with the*

> *bull's blood: He shall sprinkle it on the atonement cover and in front of it. In this way he will make atonement for the Most Holy Place because of the uncleanness and rebellion of the Israelites, whatever their sins have been (Leviticus 16:15–16).*

Much later in the Jewish Scriptures we find a strange prophecy about a man, known simply as the Lord's *servant*, whose own life would be given in a kind of Yom Kippur:

> *Surely he took up our pain and bore our suffering, yet we considered him punished by God, stricken by him, and afflicted. But he was pierced for our transgressions, he was crushed for our iniquities; the punishment that brought us peace was on him, and by his wounds we are healed. We all, like sheep, have gone astray, each of us has turned to our own way; and the Lord has laid on him the iniquity of us all (Isaiah 53:4–6).*

The passage is striking. Many scholars see it as the direct background to the early understanding of Jesus' death, and even to his own view of his suffering. A recent multi-authored book called *The Suffering Servant* is devoted to the theme.[8]

When Jesus at his Last Supper spoke of his blood as the 'blood of the covenant, which is poured out for many', he was recalling a centuries-old tradition. Mercy and judgement lay side by side in Jewish thought because both were intrinsic to the character of Israel's God. He was always willing to forgive but never at the expense of justice; he would always deal justly with evil but never without the offer of mercy. Atonement is the resolution of this tension in the heart of God. It is how he shows himself to be just towards sin yet forgiving towards the sinner. In his groundbreaking study of the historical origins of the New

Testament idea of atonement, Professor Martin Hengel of the University of Tübingen draws all of this together:

> *Jesus celebrated the Passover meal with his disciples and in it… in a symbolic action he related the broken bread to the breaking of his body and at the end of the meal the wine in the cup of blessing to the pouring out of his blood, through which the new eschatological covenant with God would be founded and atonement would be achieved for all.*[9]

Coincidentally, as I was preparing this material I read a story in the local newspaper that warrants retelling. Melbourne woman Kimberley Dear was set to fulfil a life ambition when she enrolled for skydiving lessons recently while on holiday in Missouri in the US. Her hopes were dashed when the plane she was flying in lost power and started careering towards the ground. Her instructor Robert Cook responded instantly. He apparently took hold of her and calmly talked her through what would happen next: 'As the plane is about to hit the ground, make sure you're on top of me so that I'll take the force of the impact.' They crashed. Several died, including Robert Cook. Kimberley survived and from hospital reported that in the final seconds she felt Mr Cook swivel his body into position as he pushed her head against his shoulder to cushion the blow.

I have never been a big fan of attempts – my own included – to illustrate the meaning of Jesus' death by way of modern stories. There is a danger of trivializing one or the other. But when I read of the sacrificial actions of Robert Cook – of one who gave his life to save that of another – I could not help but think of Jesus' giving of his body and blood 'for many' at the Last Supper.

10

CRUCIFIXION

What do we know of the events surrounding Jesus' death? True to form, Bishop John Shelby Spong answers, virtually nothing. He assures us that 'neither the way he died nor the events and the people who filled the story of the cross are historical'.[1] The disciples fled after Jesus' arrest, he points out, so no one was there to witness the death itself. No one knew the details. The Gospels' accounts of Jesus' suffering, known as the passion narratives, must therefore be fictional. In particular, he argues, they are attempts to cope with the disaster of Jesus' demise by fashioning a story based on Old Testament words and themes – especially Psalm 22 and Isaiah 53. That way, the whole disaster of their Master's demise can be seen as part of God's plan.

The argument no doubt reads plausibly enough to Bishop Spong's intended audience, but it does not have much currency amongst scholars.[2] For one thing, it is more than a little inconsistent to accept the Gospels' statement that the disciples fled and then ignore their references to other followers who *were* present for some of the events following Jesus' arrest. Recent scholarship has in fact drawn attention to the eyewitness roles that some of the people named in the passion narratives must have played in early Christianity.[3]

As for the allusions to the Old Testament, this is surely what we should expect from people immersed in their Bible. Virtually all scholars agree that there was an irreducible core of remembered facts about Jesus' death *and* that this was interpreted via the language and themes of the sacred Scriptures. The first disciples believed these events were of 'biblical proportions', so they reached for their Bible (the Old Testament) for a way to understand and describe them. Jews still do this. One of the proposed names for the recent thirty-four-day conflict with Hezbollah in Lebanon was 'The War to Return the Captives', an unmistakable biblical allusion to the deliverance of God's people from foreigners.[4]

Overwhelmingly, modern scholars accept as secure the broad outline of the passion narratives, from Last Supper to final breath. Few believe the entire narrative is straightforwardly accurate (as most Christians do), and a number of interesting debates continue over the details. Nevertheless, there is a strong consensus, of which Spong is unaware or defiant, that affirms at least the following few facts: Jesus shared a final meal with the twelve during the Passover week of AD 30; he was betrayed by one of the twelve; he was arrested by the Temple guards; he was interrogated by the Jewish authorities and then 'officially' tried by Pontius Pilate; after scourging, he was crucified outside the walls of Jerusalem under the charge, 'King of the Jews'.[5]

THE CRUCIFIED 'KING OF THE JEWS'?

There were probably a number of factors contributing to Jesus' arrest and execution – his clashes with the Pharisees, the rumour that he practised sorcery and his offer of forgiveness of sins without recourse to the priestly rituals. But virtually everyone writing on the topic today agrees that the immediate cause of his demise was his symbolic action of overturning the priestly tables in the Temple with its implicit (and explicit) threat of coming destruction.[6] Professor Ed Sanders of Duke University puts it memorably: 'The gun may already have been cocked, but it was the temple demonstration which pulled the trigger.'[7] This was especially the case when we remember that Jesus had entered the holy city to perform this sign by deliberately acting out the famous prophecy about the arrival of God's appointed king:

'Shout, Daughter of Jerusalem! See, your king comes to you, righteous and having salvation, gentle and riding on a donkey.'[8] Jesus' two prophetic signs that week – his regal entry into Jerusalem and his overturning of the priestly tables – amounted to a massive claim to authority. The right to rule over God's people, he was implying, rested not with the Temple leaders but with the man on the donkey, the king of Israel, the messiah.

All of this provided the Jewish elite in Jerusalem with the perfect pretext for handing over this Galilean troublemaker to the one person in town with the formal right to execute, the Roman governor Pontius Pilate. Jesus could easily be accused of being a political rebel with pretensions to kingship over Jerusalem. Here, all four Gospels agree:

> *They bound Jesus, led him away and handed him over to Pilate. 'Are you the king of the Jews?' asked Pilate. 'You have said so,' Jesus replied. The chief priests accused him of many things. So again Pilate asked him, 'Aren't you going to answer? See how many things they are accusing you of.' But Jesus still made no reply, and Pilate was amazed (Mark 15:1–5; repeated in Matthew 27:11–14 and Luke 23:2–5; independently in John 18:33–36).*

The priests no doubt knew that Jesus was no real military threat. Pilate also must have known that he commanded no army. But good order was the first concern for such leaders. Anyone stirring up crowds with claims to authority and talk of a coming kingdom was a threat to that order, especially at Passover time when Jerusalem's population swelled fourfold, religious feelings were heightened and additional Roman troops stood ready to quash any excited Jews with notions of divine liberation.[9]

And so, Jesus was tried and sentenced to death by crucifixion, the ancient world's *summum supplicium*, 'ultimate penalty'.[10] His charge, the claim to be 'King of the Jews', was placarded above the cross itself (no doubt designed to mock both Jesus and the Jews' longing for their own king). Again, on this the Gospels all agree. Perhaps no other portion of the New Testament deserves to be quoted so fully and read as poignantly:

> *They brought Jesus to the place called Golgotha (which means 'the place of the skull'). Then they offered him wine mixed with myrrh, but he did not take it. And they crucified him. Dividing up his clothes, they cast lots to see what each would get. It was nine in the morning when they crucified him. The written notice of the charge against him read: The King of the Jews. They crucified two rebels with him, one on his right and one on his left. Those who passed by hurled insults at him, shaking their heads and saying, 'So! You who are going to destroy the temple and build it in three days, come down from the cross and save yourself!' In the same way the chief priests and the teachers of the law mocked him among themselves. 'He saved others,' they said, 'but he can't save himself! Let this Messiah, this king of Israel, come down now from the cross, that we may see and believe.' Those crucified with him also heaped insults on him.*
>
> *At noon, darkness came over the whole land until three in the afternoon. And at three in the afternoon Jesus cried out in a loud voice, 'Eloi, Eloi, lema sabachthani?' (which means 'My God, my God, why have you forsaken me?'). When some of those standing near heard this, they said, 'Listen, he's calling Elijah.' Someone ran, filled a sponge with wine vinegar, put it on a staff, and offered it to Jesus to drink. 'Now leave him alone. Let's see if Elijah comes to take him down,' he said.*

With a loud cry, Jesus breathed his last. The curtain of the temple was torn in two from top to bottom. And when the centurion, who stood there in front of Jesus, saw how he died, he said, 'Surely this man was the Son of God!' Some women were watching from a distance. Among them were Mary Magdalene, Mary the mother of James the younger and of Joseph, and Salome. In Galilee these women had followed him and cared for his needs. Many other women who had come up with him to Jerusalem were also there (Mark 15:22–41; repeated with additions in Matthew 27:33–56 and Luke 23:33–49; independently in John 19:17–30).

However seriously Pilate took the priests' accusation that Jesus wanted to be 'King of the Jews', Rome could never tolerate royal claimants, especially ones with a following. Killing one man to avert even the remotest possibility of an uprising was a very small thing for a man like Pontius Pilate. He had done it before and would do so again.

All of this makes quite puzzling the attempt at historical criticism by France's most famous atheist, Professor of Philosophy Michel Onfray, in his provocative book *Atheist Manifesto*:

Another improbability: the Crucifixion. History again bears witness: at that time Jews were not crucified but stoned to death. What was Jesus accused of? Calling himself King of the Jews. The fact is that Rome could have cared less [sic] about this business of messiahs and prophecy. Crucifixion implied a challenge to the imperial power, which the crucified man never explicitly posed.[11]

Leaving aside the fact that Jews were amongst the most crucified people in antiquity, the reality is: Rome *could not have cared more* about the business of messiahs and prophecy. This was precisely the problem with the Jews. They believed in a divine king above Caesar, and they frequently got it into their heads that he wanted them to assist him in removing the Romans from the holy land. They had done this at least twice in living memory (in 4 BC and AD 6) and would do so once again in the great war of AD 66–70, which would end in the destruction of Jerusalem and its Temple.

Even if Pilate did not believe that the teacher and healer from Nazareth posed an immediate threat, nothing was more important to him than making sure the excited Jewish crowds entertained no further thoughts of an alternative kingdom. If getting rid of Jesus made this a little easier, so be it; a man like Pilate would not have equivocated. As difficult as it might be for some to imagine, in the course of Pilate's ten-year career in Palestine (AD 26–37) his order to crucify a troublemaker from Galilee under the mocking charge of 'King of the Jews' was a minor matter quickly forgotten.

JESUS' DEATH IN CHRISTIAN MEMORY

Of course, 'forgetting' was the last thing Christians could do with the death of Jesus, not just because of the horror of the event but principally because of the enormous significance they attached to it from the very beginning. Richard Dawkins may scoff 'that a religion should adopt an instrument of torture and execution as its sacred symbol, often worn around the neck',[12] but the earliest believers seem to have revelled in this deeply counter-intuitive idea. The cross instantly became the centre of their ritual life, their ethics and their theology.

It is fascinating that the only distinctive ritual of the early Christians was a celebration of Jesus' death. The so-called

Lord's Supper or Communion is a memorial meal designed to recall Jesus' own Last Supper. From the earliest days, it seems, Christians met together not just to sing songs, say prayers and listen to sermons but also to eat bread and drink wine as they recalled the words of Jesus at his final Passover meal. Paul's rendition of the Last Supper offers the earliest and clearest glimpse into this Christian ritual:

> *For I received from the Lord what I also passed on to you: The Lord Jesus, on the night he was betrayed, took bread, and when he had given thanks, he broke it and said, 'This is my body, which is for you; do this in remembrance of me.' In the same way, after supper he took the cup, saying, 'This cup is the new covenant in my blood; do this, whenever you drink it, in remembrance of me.' For whenever you eat this bread and drink this cup, you proclaim the Lord's death until he comes (1 Corinthians 11:23–26).*

Paul wrote this letter to the Corinthians in around AD 55, but it is obvious that this is not the first time he has told them about the Last Supper or urged them to rehearse it. He is reminding them of traditions already passed on to them and with which they are well accustomed. Hence, by the time of our earliest written evidence (the letters of Paul), the Communion ritual is already firmly established in the churches. The defining ritual of the early church from as early as we can discern was a meal designed to 'proclaim the Lord's death until he comes'.

The *ethical* life of the first Christians was also profoundly affected by the memory of the cross. Consider the following example from another letter of Paul dated to around AD 60 (before any of the Gospels were written). Paul quotes one of the hymns used by the early Christians to sing of Jesus' death and resurrection. What is especially striking is the way Paul introduces the song by urging his readers to model their lives on the sacrificial death of the one they sing about:

> *Do nothing out of selfish ambition or vain conceit. Rather, in humility value others above yourselves, not looking to your own interests but each of you to the interests of the others. In your relationships with one another, have the same attitude of mind Christ Jesus had:*
>
> *Who, being in very nature God,*
> *did not consider equality with God*
> *something to be used to his own advantage;*
> *rather, he made himself nothing*
> *by taking the very nature of a servant,*
> *being made in human likeness.*
> *And being found in appearance as a human being,*
> *he humbled himself by becoming obedient to death*
> *– even death on a cross!*
> *(Philippians 2:3–8)*

Just as Jesus served humanity all the way to a shameful Roman cross, so believers were to 'have the same attitude' in their daily lives. Particularly interesting for the historian of religion is the use of the word 'humility' ('in humility value others above yourselves'). Today we take for granted that humility is a desirable quality. We love it when sports stars are self-deprecating and pay tribute to their opponents. In the ancient world, however, things were very different. The word used by Paul typically meant either 'humiliation' or the *lowliness* required by ordinary folk before kings (and slaves before masters). Lowering yourself before an equal was not advisable, especially since a central goal of ancient Mediterranean life was to maximize public *honour* for yourself and your family. The first writings in antiquity clearly to emphasize humility as a central virtue were New Testament texts. And the reason seems clear. The radical idea at the centre of these texts was that the one who was 'in very nature God' deliberately 'made himself nothing'. He 'humbled himself' all the way to death, 'even death on a cross'. If the Lord of the world won his greatest achievement through the humiliation of a Roman cross, there was only one conclusion to draw: the truly good life is the life of humble sacrifice. Western culture now simply assumes this moral perspective, obscuring the fact that it is a direct inheritance from the earliest ethical reflection on the death of Jesus.

Finally, I should make clear that the cross has been central to Christian *theology* from the very beginning. Our evidence here is surprisingly strong. In Paul's first letter to the Corinthians we find a passage (15:3–5) that scholars confidently date to 'within months of Jesus' death'.[13] The letter itself was written around AD 55, but the truly significant thing is that he quotes a summary of Christian belief, a creed, that he had passed on to them for memorization five years earlier and that he himself had received for memorization when he was first being schooled in the Christian faith (that puts us in the early to mid-30s). Paul says this creed was passed on to him 'as of first importance':

> *that Christ died for our sins*
> *according to the Scriptures,*
> *that he was buried,*
> *that he was raised on the third day*
> *according to the Scriptures,*
> *and that he appeared to Cephas,*
> *and then to the Twelve.*
> *(1 Corinthians 15:3–5)*

We will reflect again on this creed in the final chapter. Here I just want to point out that the earliest piece of Christian theology – or 'doctrine' – states in no uncertain terms that Jesus 'died for our sins according to the Scriptures'. We can say with historical certainty that within a few years of the crucifixion the leading disciples, who were the only ones with the authority to compose such a creed, were proclaiming Jesus' death as a sacrifice for sins and seeing it as the fulfilment of 'the Scriptures' – that is, the Old Testament.

The early conviction that the brutal crucifixion of Jesus was in fact the means of atonement for the sins of the world had an incalculable impact on the rituals, ethics and theology of the infant church. What for Pilate was a minor matter soon forgotten was for the first Christians the centre – the crux – of God's gracious dealings in the world.

11

RESURRECTION

For many, it is a strange thought to contemplate that, if we were transported back in time to Jerusalem in AD 29, we would quickly discover that Jesus of Nazareth was not the most revered religious figure of the period. Far more famous were the names Honi the Circle-drawer,[1] who died around 65 BC, or Rabbis Hillel and Shammai, who died when Jesus was a boy. These men had captured the attention and affection of countless thousands of Jews in ancient times. Hillel and Shammai founded the two prominent 'schools' of ancient Judaism, and Honi had been a revered holy man and glorious martyr, killed for refusing to curse his own people.[2]

And, yet, today the names Honi, Hillel and Shammai are virtually unknown, and the name Jesus is recognized by untold millions throughout the world. I would venture to say that even amongst Jews today more is known about Jesus of Nazareth than any of these other Jewish luminaries.[3]

Why is this? How is it that a relatively marginal Jewish teacher and healer from Galilee came to eclipse every other religious figure of his era?

At one level, the correct answer is: the proselytizing success of the early church. But that would be to miss a more fundamental point. The thing that launched the church, that lit the fuse of its unprecedented missionary zeal, was the resurrection of Jesus – or, to put it more acceptably for the historian, the *belief* in the resurrection of Jesus. The first Christians were utterly convinced that their Lord had been raised to life by God, and this conviction gave them an unparalleled resolve to take his words and deeds to the ends of the earth. We live in the wake of that.

But what can a historian *speaking as a historian* say about this cornerstone of Christian conviction?

SCHOLARLY DISCUSSION ABOUT THE RESURRECTION

The first thing to note is that quite a bit *is* actually said on the subject. An annotated bibliography of the historical Jesus research published almost twenty years ago lists no fewer than ninety-four academic books and journal articles devoted to the resurrection.[4] A decade later Oxford University published the papers of an international scholarly symposium on the subject, combining a range of relevant disciplines – history and philosophy as well as theology.[5] A great many more books and articles have since appeared. And, please be clear, I am not talking about the work of Christian apologists and seminary professors (which would inflate the numbers considerably[6]) but that of professional New Testament historians, of varying beliefs themselves, many of whom hold the chairs at leading secular universities around the world. I am thinking especially of Professors Graham Stanton of the University of Cambridge, James Dunn of the Durham University, Gerd Theissen and Annette Merz of the University of Heidelberg, Marcus Bockmuehl of the University of St Andrews, Ed Sanders of Duke University and others.[7]

All of these scholars agree that there is an irreducible historical core to the resurrection story that cannot be explained away as pious legend or wholesale deceit. Professor Sanders, who warms a seat at the sceptical end of mainstream scholarship, states things plainly: 'That Jesus' followers (and later Paul) had resurrection experiences is, in my judgement, a fact. What the reality was that gave rise to the experiences I do not know.'[8] This is typical of the secular study of Jesus: something very strange happened; we just don't quite know what!

Less equivocal but no less scholarly is the massive recent work of British New Testament scholar N. T. Wright, called *The*

Resurrection of the Son of God. His conclusion is compelling, if understated: 'The proposal that Jesus was bodily raised from the dead possesses unrivalled power to explain the historical data at the heart of early Christianity.'[9] Put another way, there is a resurrection-shaped 'dent' in the historical record (most would agree with him on that); and only the actual bodily resurrection of Jesus satisfactorily explains it (here, most historians prefer to plead ignorance). Wright cannot really be classed as a 'secular' scholar – he is the current Bishop of Durham! – but his 800-page tome is universally regarded as the most important historical work ever written on the subject. (Not that his ecclesiastical position should matter. Other church luminaries – Bishop Spong, for instance – have had well-publicized doubts about the resurrection.[10])

None of this is intended to convince readers that the resurrection is true (I do not believe it is possible to prove the resurrection). That a number of clever people continue to discuss this topic proves nothing. Here, I am simply trying to illustrate what is rarely noted in popular discussions about Jesus. The resurrection remains a serious topic of academic investigation today. It is not a theme confined to churches and theological seminaries; it is a serious subject of historical investigation.

THE 'FACT' BEHIND THE RESURRECTION

Several things about the resurrection of Jesus can be affirmed with a degree of historical confidence. For instance, it is generally agreed that Jesus' tomb was empty shortly after his burial and that Jews in the period had no pre-existing expectation about a 'risen messiah' which might have inspired claims about Jesus (quite the opposite, in fact).[11] But there is one detail that is regarded as *certain* by virtually every scholar writing on the subject today. From the very beginning, numbers of men and women claimed to have seen Jesus alive after death. That eyewitnesses testified to resurrection appearances is a fact of history. Professor James Dunn of Durham University, one of the leading New Testament historians of the last two decades, puts the matter plainly:

> *What we should recognize as beyond reasonable doubt is that the first believers experienced 'resurrection appearances' and that those experiences are enshrined, as with the earlier impact made by Jesus' teaching and actions, in the traditions which have come down to us.*[12]

The most significant evidence of the witnesses to the resurrection is found in the passage from Paul's letter to the Corinthians quoted in the previous chapter. I have already explained that the importance of this text for the historian is that it contains a fixed summary of Christian belief (a creed) that can be dated to the early to mid-30s AD. It deserves to be quoted again:

> *Now, brothers and sisters, I want to remind you of the gospel I preached to you, which you received and on which you have taken your stand. By this gospel you are saved, if you hold firmly to the word I preached to you. Otherwise, you have believed in vain. For what I received I passed on to you as of first importance:*
>
> *that Christ died for our sins*
> * according to the Scriptures,*
> *that he was buried,*
> *that he was raised on the third day*
> * according to the Scriptures,*
> *and that he appeared to Cephas,*
> * and then to the Twelve.*

> *After that, he appeared to more than five hundred of the brothers and sisters at the same time, most of whom are still living, though some have fallen asleep. Then he appeared to James, then to all the apostles, and last of all he appeared to me also, as to one abnormally born (1 Corinthians 15:1–8).*

Just about every one of the twenty-seven documents in the New Testament bears indirect testimony to the fact that eyewitnesses claimed to have seen Jesus alive after his death, but this passage is on another level entirely. For one thing, the early date of the creed (indented above) rules out the popular idea that the resurrection story was a slowly developing legend. Even scholars who absolutely rule out the possibility of a resurrection admit that the reports in this creed come from the period almost immediately after the purported event itself and cannot be the result of legendary accumulation.[13]

There are six witnesses, or groups of witnesses, listed here by Paul:

1. Cephas – the Aramaic version of Peter.
2. The twelve – that is, the authorized group of Jesus' apostles (including Peter and Judas' replacement, Matthias[14]).
3. The group of 500 'brothers and sisters' – probably a reference to an extended group of Christians, most of whom were still alive in AD 55 when Paul wrote to the Corinthians.
4. James – the brother of Jesus who wrote one of the letters of the New Testament and who also features in the book of Acts.
5. 'All of the apostles' – a larger group of missionaries beyond the symbolically charged twelve.
6. Paul – something of a late-comer, as he admits.

Despite this self-deprecation, Paul's testimony amounts to firsthand eyewitness testimony. We have to confront this. The historian has to ask: how did a fanatical persecutor of the Christian movement suddenly become a promoter of the news of the resurrection? It is a historical puzzle all of its own.

Much more could be said about 1 Corinthians 15 but I want to add to this list another group of witnesses Paul does not mention but which modern historians regard as equally early and authentic. In different ways, all four Gospels agree that the first people to learn of the empty tomb and the risen Jesus were not the male apostles but the *women* who had travelled with him from Galilee to Jerusalem. The account of Mary Magdalene in John's Gospel is perhaps the most vivid:

> *Early on the first day of the week, while it was still dark, Mary Magdalene went to the tomb and saw that the stone had been removed from the entrance... At this, she turned around and saw Jesus standing there, but she did not realize that it was Jesus. He asked her, 'Woman, why are you crying? Who is it you are looking for?' Thinking he was the gardener, she said, 'Sir, if you have carried him away, tell me where you have put him, and I will get him.' Jesus said to her, 'Mary.' She turned toward him and cried out in Aramaic, 'Rabboni!' (which means 'Teacher'). Jesus said, 'Do not hold on to me, for I have not yet ascended to the Father. Go instead to my brothers and tell them, "I am ascending to my Father and your Father, to my God and your God."' Mary Magdalene went to the disciples with the news: 'I have seen the Lord!' And she told them that he had said these things to her (John 20:1–18; see also Mark 16:1–8; Matthew 28:1–8; Luke 24:1–12, 22–23).*

Of the women at the tomb Professor James Dunn (Durham University) says, 'This is one of the firmest features of the tradition in all its variation.' And, yet, 'as is well known, in Middle Eastern society of the time women were not regarded as reliable witnesses: a woman's testimony in court was heavily discounted'.[15] The significance of the observations is obvious. Unless it was well known from the beginning that the first people to witness the empty tomb and the resurrection were women, why would all four Gospel writers include the detail in their accounts, leaving themselves wide open to criticism from their contemporaries on just this point? These authors, says Professor Graham Stanton of the University of Cambridge, 'were well aware of customary attitudes to the testimony of women, but they simply recorded the traditions they received, even though they would have carried little weight in arguments with opponents'.[16] This is perhaps an understatement. We know that one of the stinging criticisms levelled against the resurrection story by second-century sceptics was precisely that it depended on the testimony of 'a hysterical female'.[17] Put simply, if you were making up a story about a resurrection and you wanted your fellow first-century Jews to believe it, you would not include women as the initial witnesses, unless it happened embarrassingly to be the case. For this reason (another example of the 'criterion of embarrassment'), scholars regard the report of the women's testimony, along with that of the male disciples, as early and authentic.[18]

FACTS, ASSUMPTIONS AND PREFERENCES

So, it is a 'fact' that from the beginning multiple witnesses – men and women – claimed that they saw Jesus alive from the dead. But what explains this fact? Some noted scholars have made a forceful case that only an *actual* resurrection adequately explains all the data (for example, N. T. Wright, quoted earlier).

But most stop short of this, preferring a kind of scholarly agnosticism. The more common approach is that of Professor Ed Sanders, mentioned previously: 'That Jesus' followers (and later Paul) had resurrection experiences is, in my judgement, a fact. What the reality was that gave rise to the experiences I do not know.'[19] I personally think that Wright has the stronger overall argument, but I also recognize that his line of reasoning involves both philosophy and history.

As with the topic of healings discussed in Chapter 7, how we interpret historical data about things 'supernatural' depends significantly on our prior philosophical assumptions. If I am convinced that the laws of nature are the only things regulating the universe – that there is no law-giver behind these laws – then I will refuse to accept *any* evidence as sufficient to demonstrate the occurrence of a 'miracle', whether a healing or a resurrection. I will either seek a naturalistic explanation of the data, however implausible that explanation might be, or I will plead ignorance. In the case of Jesus' healings, historians usually opt for the second approach. Very, very few try to explain the evidence. Instead, they conclude simply that Jesus did things that his contemporaries believed to be miraculous. This approach, as we saw, is adopted even by those who reject the possibility of miracles.

A similar situation pertains to the resurrection. Surprisingly few scholars attempt naturalistic explanations, such as that the disciples stole the body and kept quiet about it to their deaths or that they experienced multiple independent hallucinations over a period of months. Instead, they adopt Sanders' stance: *something strange happened, we just don't know what*! As I said earlier, there is a resurrection-shaped 'dent' in this historical record that cannot reasonably be denied. What explains the dent is a matter that goes beyond strictly historical considerations. The atheist will find no great comfort in the historical data – it is not nearly as vacuous as he or she might have hoped. But nor will the Christian find any proof there. In any case, what kind of proof could there ever be for a miracle in the past? How each of us interprets the evidence about the resurrection will involve our prior philosophical assumptions and, perhaps above all, our personal reflections.

This point is well made in the thoroughly untrue anecdote a friend once told me. A man woke up one morning convinced he was dead. His wife thought he was joking and cheekily asked how he could be *talking* about being dead. But it soon became clear that he was serious: he was dead. After various attempts to convince him otherwise, she finally invited a brilliant psychiatrist to interview him and try to remedy the situation. No change. Eventually, the psychiatrist had an idea. He opened one of his weighty medical texts and pointed his patient to one of the incontrovertible facts about dead people: they do not bleed. 'With the heart stopping and the blood coagulating,' he said slowly and precisely, 'a dead body can no longer bleed.' The evidence was compelling and the man agreed: dead people certainly do not bleed. At this moment the psychiatrist reached for a pin and thrust it into the patient's forearm. Blood shot straight up like a tiny fountain. Astonished the man looked at his arm and exclaimed, 'Well, what do you know, dead people do bleed after all!'

My point is not that the evidence for the resurrection is equal to that relating to blood flow in a corpse (it certainly is not). I am merely illustrating that often *evidence* is not the only factor in our life decisions. Intellectual assumptions and personal inclinations often play a significant part. The challenge of Jesus' resurrection is not simply a historical one (though for some it begins there). It is also one that invites us to examine our convictions about the world and about the existence of God.

EPILOGUE

A SHORT LIFE?

THE 'AFTERMATH' OF JESUS

In discussing the women in Jesus' life I recalled the caution sounded by Professor Paula Fredriksen of Boston University against too quickly searching for the modern significance of Jesus: 'the more facile the ethical or political relevance that a particular construct of Jesus presents, the more suspect its worth as history'.[1] The warning is a good one, particularly for an author writing a book on Jesus for a general twenty-first-century readership. The question of Jesus' ongoing significance for modern life, then, is not easily answered, at least not without sounding a little facile and sermonic.

Nevertheless, I am buoyed by the approach of several eminent scholars, notably Ed Sanders of Duke University and Graham Stanton at Cambridge, who argue that it is perfectly appropriate for the historian to explore what they call the 'aftermath' of Jesus. While the study of the historical Jesus is its own discrete topic, his words and deeds had an enormous, long-lasting impact on the communities of his followers. And this impact can be studied historically.[2] We can actually observe in ancient texts the way the early Christians wrestled with the implications of the Jesus-event in their new situation. They did not look back on Jesus' short life with simple nostalgia; they saw their work as an extension of his. Sanders describes them as 'carrying through the logic of his [Jesus'] own position in a transformed situation'.[3]

Taking my cue from this line of reasoning, I want briefly to point out some of the more important connections between the historical Jesus and early Christian practice and belief. It is here that we will find points of ongoing 'relevance' for twenty-first-century readers that are hopefully neither facile nor sermonic.

THE SIMPLIFICATION OF 'RELIGION'

Jesus' critique of the Pharisees' 'traditions of the elders' and of the Temple system seems to have left its mark on the first Christians. One of the most striking features of the New Testament is its step *away* from mainstream Judaism – away from concerns about ritual purity, away from detailed analysis of the requirements of God's law and away from any significant role for the Temple. Don't misunderstand me. The first Christians still thought of themselves as Jews. They also met and prayed in the Temple and frequently quoted from the Jewish Scriptures (the Old Testament).[4] But a comparison of the New Testament with any of the other Jewish writings of the period reveals some very clear differences. One of the most obvious is the absence of an interest in food laws, Temple sacrifices and legal rulings. Even a book such as James, written to fellow Jewish believers, shows no concern for such issues. Devotion to the teachings of Jesus, especially to his ethic of love, takes centre stage. James describes this new way of life as 'the perfect law that gives freedom'.[5]

I do not doubt that over time the Christian church has found ways to replace the traditions of the Pharisees with traditions of its own, but the faith that Jesus established has an in-built critique of the human tendency to *add* to God's ways. Jesus' words to his opponents have a continuing resonance: 'You have let go of the commands of God and are holding on to human traditions.'[6] There is, in other words, a theoretical simplicity to Christian living, perfectly expressed in a comment of the apostle Paul to the Galatians: 'For in Christ Jesus neither circumcision nor uncircumcision has any value. The only thing that counts is faith expressing itself through love.'[7] Jesus' radicalization of love, making it the absolute centre of the religious life and demanding that it encompass our enemies as well as our neighbours, is one of his most profound and lasting contributions to the history of ideas. Many who have little time for formal religion today still find themselves attracted to the beauty and simplicity of this vision.

A FAITH FOR THE WHOLE WORLD

The above quotation from Paul highlights a related issue. Perhaps the most dramatic shift in early Christianity was the decision in the 40s AD to allow non-Jews, Gentiles, full admission into the Christian community without having to become Jews through circumcision.[8] This was a true paradigm shift, and it transformed this fledgling Jewish renewal movement into the world religion we know as Christianity.

Jesus had said nothing about circumcision and he had minimal contact with Gentiles, so, in a sense, the early Christians were on their own in this decision. But Graham Stanton is surely right to suggest that, while the disciples had no specific saying of Jesus on the question, they did have powerful memories of his scandalous table-fellowship with sinners and tax collectors (discussed in Chapter 6). It was no giant leap, then, to conclude that the grace of Christ towards the 'outsider' should extend even to Gentiles without them first having to become Jews. Reflecting on this theme the apostle Paul wrote, 'There is neither Jew nor Gentile, neither slave nor free, neither male nor female, for you are all one in Christ Jesus.'[9] This universalistic spirit has not always been present amongst the followers of Jesus through the centuries but it is certainly a striking feature of New Testament spirituality, and I venture to say that it is one with important implications today.

FORGIVENESS OF SINS

No theme of Jesus' life has more ongoing appeal than that of the forgiveness of sins. This was not a uniquely Christian idea, of course. As Professor Ed Sanders has reminded scholars over the years, forgiveness was deeply embedded within Judaism long before it was found in Christian Scripture.[10] That said, it is beyond doubt that Jesus adopted a surprisingly lavish and direct approach to divine mercy. He bypassed the normal priestly protocols of the day and handed out forgiveness to the guilty as if it were his to give. 'Why does this fellow talk like that?' asked his detractors. 'Who can forgive sins but God alone?'[11]

As we saw in Chapter 9, Jesus spoke of his death as the means of liberation from the coming judgement – a kind of Passover sacrifice. The early Christians crystallized this motif, affirming in their earliest datable creed, 'that Christ died for our sins according to the Scriptures'.[12] Divine judgement has always been a feature of Christian proclamation – as it was with Jesus – but alongside this 'bad news' stands the very, very good news, the 'gospel', that the unworthy and condemned can have full assurance of God's pardon through Jesus. For me, the 'aftermath' of Jesus is felt nowhere more keenly than in the ongoing message of divine forgiveness in his name. In the modern world, acceptance typically comes on the basis of achievement – whether in the playground, in physical appearance, on the sporting field, in business or in academia. But what we find in Jesus, says the New Testament, is a lavish and direct path to divine acceptance.

WORKING FOR THE 'KINGDOM COME'

One of Ed Sanders' 'secure facts about the aftermath of Jesus' life' is that his disciples 'believed that he would return to found the kingdom' and that 'they formed a community to await his return'.[13] Central to the legacy of Jesus was an expectation of a future kingdom in which justice would reign and creation would be restored. We have seen that Jesus viewed his healings and exorcisms as signs of that kingdom. Restoring the blind and the lame and ridding people of the forces of darkness in their lives were a kind of preview of God's future restoration of all things. The early Christians continued to treasure this theme.

Historically, this longing for the return of Christ and the establishment of his kingdom led to two opposite tendencies within the church. Some Christians over the centuries adopted an 'apocalyptic' view of the future (*apokalupsis* is Greek for 'revelation'). Here, the expectation that God will one day make everything new is thought to mean that believers should shun this condemned world, huddle in alternative communities and wait for the disclosure of the kingdom.

A second approach is, I believe, more in tune with the logic of Jesus and more consistent with the teachings of the New Testament generally. Precisely because God is coming to renew creation and restore justice believers are to work towards these realities here and now. They have glimpsed the future in the powerful deeds of Jesus; they know he will return one day to bring these things to fulfilment; and so they try to embody this future in their daily lives. They work for justice, they seek the healing of others and so on. The logic is simple: we may not yet possess all the resources of the 'kingdom come', but we do know its aims – to renew human life and put an end to evil – and these should shape what we strive for now. The sentiment is stated perfectly in the famous prayer Jesus taught his disciples, the so-called Lord's Prayer: 'your kingdom come, your will be done, on earth as it is in heaven'.[14] Hope for Christ's coming kingdom, in other words, is not 'other-worldly', pie-in-the-sky when you die. Christians know that God will one day disclose his kingdom of peace and justice. Until then, they work to fulfil his will on earth as it is in heaven. Hope for the future and action here and now: these are the perspectives Jesus expected his followers to embrace.

ONE TO WORSHIP

Finally, Graham Stanton of the University of Cambridge points to a quite astonishing aspect of the 'aftermath' of Jesus. Very quickly after his death and resurrection (whatever we make of that), the disciples began to worship him in language hitherto used only for God.[15] It is sometimes wrongly suggested that Jesus was originally viewed simply as a great teacher and that magnification into a god-figure occurred centuries later. The usual story has Emperor Constantine in the fourth century playing a key role in this 'elevation' of Jesus. The story works in a novel but it has no basis in history.

Scholarship on the question of Jesus' 'divinity' has established beyond contention that *the first generation of Christians* offered prayers to Jesus and spoke of him in the same breath (and in the same terminology) as God the Father.[16] It is an extraordinary fact – and an active field of contemporary research – that these early Jewish monotheists began to worship Jesus in ways historically reserved for the Creator himself. A hymn from Paul's letter to the Philippians written in the middle of the first century (and quoted already in Chapter 10) says that, before his suffering, Jesus shared God's nature: 'Who, being in very nature God'. Moreover, after his suffering, the hymn continues, he was granted:

> *… the name that is above every name, that at the name of Jesus every knee should bow, in heaven and on earth and under the earth, and every tongue acknowledge that Jesus Christ is Lord, to the glory of God the Father (Philippians 2:6–11).*

Equally striking is a statement of Paul to the Corinthians:

> *There is but one God, the Father, from whom all things came and for whom we live; and there is but*

> *one Lord, Jesus Christ, through whom all things came and through whom we live (1 Corinthians 8:6).*

Commenting on this passage Graham Stanton writes: 'Here statements about God and Christ are not merely juxtaposed, they are carefully set out in parallel. How could all this have happened if Jesus of Nazareth was merely a sage or a conventional teacher?'[17] Stanton's answer, accepted by most writing on the subject today, is that Jesus never presented himself merely as a sage. He often spoke of himself in such lofty terms that it was almost inevitable that those closest to him would begin to think of him in exalted terms. For one thing, as Ed Sanders says, 'Jesus taught his disciples that he himself would play the principal role in the kingdom.'[18] This instantly places him in a category altogether different from that of the rabbis and priests of his day. His selection of the twelve as a symbol of Israel points in the same direction. We noted in Chapter 6 that Jesus was not thought to be part of that group – it was not eleven + Jesus. He stood apart from it and over it. The twelve were *his* representatives. This was a claim to maximum authority in Israel. Then there was his entry into Jerusalem on a donkey (recalling a prophecy about the arrival of God's king), combined with his symbolic action against the Temple. As I said in Chapter 8, these actions were intended to imply that the right to rule over God's people rested not with the Temple leaders but with the man on the donkey. Moreover, his offer of forgiveness independent of cultic rituals and his explicit statement that the national shrine was doomed to destruction suggest that he even placed himself above the Temple itself, the embodiment of God's presence and mercy on earth.

Ultimately, all of these things were interpreted by the disciples in the dazzling light of the resurrection. Whatever we make of the resurrection today, it is certain that the first disciples experienced what they held to be appearances of the risen Christ.

And it was this experience, above all, that convinced them that 'at the name of Jesus every knee should bow'.[19] Without the resurrection experiences, Jesus' name would have been no more significant than that of Honi – that other great Jewish martyr from the period, revered for a while, then forgotten. But the conviction about the risen Jesus changed everything. It instantly became the core and premise of the entire movement. It was the reason for the confession, 'Jesus Christ is Lord.'

THE LIMITS OF HISTORY AND FAITH

The call to 'bow the knee' to Jesus – to offer him the worship due to the Creator – is either the most ludicrous part of the aftermath of Jesus or the most relevant. But which of these we judge it to be is not really a historical matter. By definition, history cannot discern Jesus' (or anyone else's) connection to God. Such things involve philosophical considerations and personal judgements. This is why I said at the outset of the book that the content of this work, which restricts itself to what can be demonstrated historically, in no way encompasses all that I hold to be true about Jesus. I passionately affirm the statement in Paul's hymn above but I also know that it cannot be verified by any historical method. History cannot prove Christianity or convince anyone to worship the crucified and risen Jesus. In this sense, my beloved academic discipline has limited relevance to Christian faith.

On the other hand, a faith that so boldly affirms that certain events took place in datable history should expect that intelligent people are going to ask historical questions. For it would be utterly incredible if a story like the one told in the Gospels allowed no possibility of historical substantiation: no external writings corroborating the broad outline, no internal sources offering multiple attestation, no physical details confirmed by archaeology and no cultural peculiarities firmly locating it in a recognizable time and place. It should be obvious to readers by now that the New Testament portrait of Jesus has all of these and more.

By no means can all (or even most) of the particulars of the story of Jesus be confirmed: some details, such as the virgin birth, have no possibility of verification and others, such as the nativity in Bethlehem, have insufficient evidence to arrive at a historical decision. Nevertheless, there is very wide agreement amongst contemporary scholars – whether Christian, Jewish or agnostic – that we do in fact know quite a bit about Jesus. Virtually everyone agrees that we know at least the following:

- when and where he lived;
- that he started out within the orbit of John the Baptist;
- that he was famous in his day as a teacher and healer;
- that he proclaimed the kingdom of God and warned of a looming catastrophe in Israel;
- that he insisted on a radicalized ethic of love;
- that he selected a group of twelve to symbolize a renewed Israel;
- that he attracted many women into his circle and was notorious for dining with sinners;
- that he caused a major, albeit symbolic, disturbance in the Temple;
- that he shared a final meal with his disciples during Passover;
- that he was handed over to Pontius Pilate by the priestly elite;
- that he was crucified under the mocking charge of 'King of the Jews';

- that numerous men and women insisted they saw him alive shortly after his death;
- and, finally, that these followers established communities that looked forward to Christ's kingdom and sought to win Jews and Gentiles to that vision.

Plenty of other details are considered either *probable* or *plausible*, but these are the acknowledged *facts* about the historical Jesus. Doubting them requires an arbitrary type of scepticism insensitive to historical method and consensus.

The list of accepted facts about Jesus makes it apparent that the Christian's decision to bow the knee to Christ is not inconsistent with the evidence. At the same time, it is perfectly clear that the facts are not sufficient to demand such a move. There is an obvious gap between what we know of the historical Jesus and what believers affirm about their risen Lord. The gap is probably not as wide as some think, but it is real. Hence, the move from a factual knowledge of Jesus to a sincere faith in him involves a significant step, sometimes pejoratively called a 'leap'.

The move from facts to faith is not unlike the 'leap' implicit in the decision to marry (I am encouraged here by the frequent analogy drawn in the New Testament between marriage and Christian faith[20]). The period of courtship does not provide the 'evidence' (if that's the right word) that a relationship can be sustained 'for better, for worse, for richer, for poorer, as long as we both shall live'. The earliest stages of young love can only ever offer indications of compatibility, hints of what might unfold in the years to come. Those indications will no doubt be *consistent* with the decision to devote your life to another, but they will not demand that step. Does this make the decision to marry irrational or ill-advised? Some might think so, but most of us still believe that an exclusive, life-long pledge to a partner – whether formal or informal – is a reasonable, beautiful and compelling step to take. We understand that something mysterious goes on, beyond the level of evidence. The courtship of course provides *reasons* for marrying but, just as importantly, it also generates deep emotions, physical passions and an inexplicable 'resonance' with the beloved. Having recently acted as a celebrant for some dear friends, I have a very clear sense as I write this of the potency of this combination of factors leading two people to make their vows.

My point is probably obvious. History can only ever hope to provide 'indications' of the reality of Christian faith. It demonstrates that the story at the heart of the Gospels is neither a myth nor a fraud, but a broadly credible account of a short first-century life. Such indications are certainly consistent with the decision to devote oneself to the risen Christ but they in no way compel that step. Other, more mysterious, factors also come into play; and to explore these would be to go beyond history into mystery.

NOTES

INTRODUCTION. WHY THE HEADLINES ALMOST ALWAYS GET HIM WRONG

1 Cornelius Tacitus (AD 56–120), *Annals* 15.44.

2 Friends insist that a '*Da Vinci Code* cringe' has set in amongst the public. The mere mention of the book/film apparently arouses some embarrassment that we were all so enamoured with it for a while.

3 For further details see Tom Wright's *Judas and the Gospel of Jesus*. SPCK, 2006.

4 Jeffrey Archer, *The Gospel According to Judas, by Benjamin Iscariot*. Macmillan, 2007.

5 John Shelby Spong, *Jesus for the Non-Religious*. HarperCollins, 2007.

6 Reading the Gospels as 'midrash' – a form of pious Jewish story telling with a metaphorical point – was proposed thirty years ago by Michael D. Goulder, *Midrash and Lection in Matthew*. London: SPCK, 1974. It has almost no currency in mainstream scholarship today, for two reasons. First, studies of Jewish midrash reveal many more differences than similarities between this Jewish form of writing and the Gospels. Secondly, as we will see in Chapter 3, the Gospels can now be firmly placed within the genre of Graeco-Roman biography. In light of this, Bishop Spong's metaphorical reading of the Gospels is simply untenable. He is free to dismiss as many Gospel stories as he likes, but it is disingenuous to claim that the writers of these texts never intended them to be read as history. A multi-authored volume dedicated to the question of the Gospels' connection to midrash is R. T. France and David Wenham (editors), *Gospel Perspectives, Volume 3: Studies in Midrash and Historiography*. Wipf & Stock, 2003.

7 E. P. Sanders, *The Historical Figure of Jesus*. Penguin Books, 1993, 11.

8 Philip Jenkins, *Hidden Gospels: How the Search for Jesus Lost its Way*. Oxford University Press, 2001.

9 Richard Dawkins, *The God Delusion*. Bantam Press, 2006, 96–97, 250.

10 My Muslim friends are quick to point out to me that the New Testament is a compilation of personal letters, biographical material, historical narrative and sermonic material, whereas the Quran contains

only the divine first person, the voice of Allah. According to Islamic theology, the prophet Muhammad had no role in determining the words of the Quran. He was simply a conduit. He heard the revelation through the angel Gabriel and transmitted it to his disciples. Such a thing has never been claimed for the writers of the New Testament. Their individual 'voices' are plainly heard throughout – so that scholars can talk about the 'Lukan style' or 'Pauline vocabulary'.

CHAPTER 1. JESUS ON THE MARGINS OF HISTORY

1 'Having said this, he spat on the ground, made some mud with the saliva, and put it on the man's eyes. "Go," he told him, "wash in the Pool of Siloam" (this word means "Sent"). So the man went and washed, and came home seeing' (John 9:6–7).

2 The news was announced to the world in three articles in the *Jerusalem Post*: 10 June 2004, page 5; 25 June 2004, page 12; 24 December 2004, page 6.

3 Details of the Siloam pool are reported in Urban C. von Wahlde, 'Archaeology and John's Gospel' (523–586) in *Jesus and Archaeology* (edited by James H. Charlesworth). Eerdmans, 2006, 568–570.

4 John Dominic Crossan, 'Parable' (146–152) in *The Anchor Bible Dictionary*, vol.5. Doubleday, 1992, 146.

5 The United Nations World Population Profile 2003 indicates that there are 2,069,883,000 (just over two billion) Christians in the world spread across 238 countries.

6 John P. Meier, *A Marginal Jew: rethinking the historical Jesus* (in three volumes). Doubleday, 1991–2001. This quote is from volume one, page 7.

7 John Dickson, *The Christ Files: how historians know what they know about Jesus*. Blue Bottle Books, 2005. See also the excellent introduction to these issues by Boston University's Professor Howard Clark Kee, *What Can We Know about Jesus?* Cambridge University Press, 1990.

8 *Jewish Antiquities* 20.200. The translation is that of Louis H. Feldman (Loeb Classical Library vol.456. Harvard University Press, 1996).

9 The brothers of Jesus are named in Mark 6:3. Their travels as missionaries are referred to in 1 Corinthians 9:5. James' leadership of the Jerusalem church is mentioned in Acts 15:13; 21:18 and in Galatians 1:19; 2:9.

10 The original Syriac and translation are found in W. Cureton, *Spicilegium Syriacum*. London: Francis and John Rivington, 1855.
11 See further, Gerd Theissen and Annette Merz, *The Historical Jesus: a comprehensive guide*. Fortress Press, 1998, 77; Craig A. Evans, *Noncanonical Writings and New Testament Interpretation*. Hendrickson, 1992, 171.
12 Tacitus, *Annals* 15.44.
13 Christopher Tuckett, 'Sources and Methods' in *The Cambridge Companion to Jesus* (edited by Marcus Bockmuehl). Cambridge University Press, 2001, 124.
14 Richard Dawkins, *The God Delusion*. Bantam Press, 2006, 97.
15 *Conspiracy Theory: Did We Land on the Moon?* (Nash Entertainment, 2001).

CHAPTER 2. HOW HISTORIANS READ THE NEW TESTAMENT

1 See the careful historical discussions of the Gnostic Gospels in John P. Meier, *A Marginal Jew: rethinking the historical Jesus* [vol.1]. Doubleday, 1991, 112–141; Gerd Theissen and Annette Merz, *The Historical Jesus: a comprehensive guide*. Fortress Press, 1998, 37–43, 47–54; Robert Van Voorst, *Jesus Outside the New Testament: An Introduction to the Ancient Evidence*. Eerdmans, 2000, 179–217; James Dunn, *Jesus Remembered*. Eerdmans, 2003, 161–165, 167–172; Graham Stanton, *The Gospels and Jesus* (Second Edition). Oxford University Press, 2003, 122–139.
2 The translation is that of Beate Blatz in *New Testament Apocrypha, vol. 1: Gospels and Related Writings* (edited by Wilhelm Schneemelcher). James Clarke & Co. Ltd, 1991.
3 About five sayings in the Gospel of Thomas are often thought to go back to Jesus: 42, 81, 82, 97, 98. 'While the historian must always be grateful for new scraps of evidence, these five sayings hardly mark a dramatic advance.' Graham Stanton, *The Gospels and Jesus* (Second Edition). Oxford University Press, 2003, 129.
4 Richard Dawkins, *The God Delusion*. Bantam Press, 2006, 95.
5 On the question of the early authority of the four New Testament Gospels see the excellent book by University of Tübingen's Professor Martin Hengel, *The Four Gospels and the One Gospel of Jesus Christ*. Trinity Press, 2000.
6 See the measured conclusion of John P. Meier, *A Marginal Jew: rethinking the historical Jesus* [vol.1]. Doubleday, 1991, 140–141.

7 You can read his own account in Galatians 1:13–20.

8 The precise date of each of Paul's letters is not known but it is certain that he wrote between AD 50 and 64. On the chronology of Paul see Rainer Riesner, *Paul's Early Period: Chronology, Mission Strategy, Theology*. Eerdmans, 1998. The historical source for the martyrdom of Paul (by beheading) is Eusebius, *Ecclesiastical History* 2.25.5–6. There is no reason to doubt the account.

9 Richard Dawkins, *The God Delusion*. Bantam Press, 2006, 93.

10 John Shelby Spong, *Jesus for the Non-Religious*. HarperCollins, 2007, 157.

11 The pivotal work on this question was by Richard Burridge, *What are the Gospels? A Comparison With Graeco-Roman Biography*. Cambridge University Press, 1992.

12 Samuel Byrskog, *Story as History, History as Story: The Gospel Tradition in the Context of Ancient Oral History*. Brill Academic Publishers, 2002.

13 Richard Bauckham, *Jesus and the Eyewitnesses*. Eerdmans, 2006.

14 There are two important pieces of evidence: (1) by making Peter the first disciple named in his work (Mark 1:16) and the last (Mark 16:7) Mark creates an *inclusio*, literary bookends, designed to specify who his eyewitness source was, a practice used by other ancient authors and referred to as the *inclusio of eyewitness testimony*; (2) in a very early writing Papias of Heirapolis (AD 60–130) directly affirms Mark's dependence on Peter's testimony in Eusebius, *Ecclesiastical History* 3.39.15. For scholarly accounts of these arguments see: Richard Bauckham, *Jesus and the Eyewitnesses*. Eerdmans, 2006, 155–182, 202–239; Martin Hengel, *The Four Gospels and the One Gospel of Jesus Christ*. Trinity Press, 2000, 65–89.

15 Throughout this discussion of the sources within the Gospels (Q, L and so on) I have been following the very balanced account of Robert Van Voorst, *Jesus Outside the New Testament: An Introduction to the Ancient Evidence*. Eerdmans, 2000.

16 See the groundbreaking study by James Dunn, *Jesus Remembered*. Eerdmans, 2003, particularly pages 173–254. Another important name in the discussion of oral tradition is Birger Gerhardsson, *The Reliability of the Gospel Tradition*. Hendrickson, 2001.

17 It should be obvious that when a passage from Mark appears also in Matthew and Luke, this is not multiple attestation; it is simply repetition. Matthew and Luke have simply copied their Markan source. On the importance of the criterion of multiple attestation for

the study of history see John P. Meier, *A Marginal Jew: rethinking the historical Jesus* [vol.1]. Doubleday, 1991, 174–175.
18 Graham Stanton, *The Gospels and Jesus* (Second Edition). Oxford University Press, 2003, 295.

CHAPTER 3. VITAL STATISTICS

1 Matthew 2:1; Luke 1:5.
2 The very sorry tale of this despot's demise is recorded by Josephus, *Jewish Antiquities* 17.173–199.
3 See Luke 3:1 and Luke 3:23.
4 BC, of course, stands for *before* Christ.
5 John P. Meier, 'Reflections on Jesus-of-history research today' (84–107) in James Charlesworth (editor), *Jesus' Jewishness*. Crossroad, 1991, 87.
6 Matthew 2:1; Luke 2:4.
7 John Shelby Spong, *Jesus for the Non-Religious*. HarperCollins, 2007, 15.
8 Raymond E. Brown, *The Birth of the Messiah*. Cassell & Collier Macmillan, 1977, especially pages 513–516.
9 See the wonderful first-century eyewitness account of Galilee in Josephus, *Jewish War* 3.42–43.
10 See, for example, Sean Freyne, *Jesus, a Jewish Galilean: A New Reading of the Jesus-Story*. T & T Clark, 2005.
11 For this and other passages from Q, the first Gospel reference is the one quoted; the second is the parallel account.
12 On the clash with the empire see, Sean Freyne, *Jesus, a Jewish Galilean: A New Reading of the Jesus-Story*. T & T Clark, 2005, 122–149. In 4 BC Herod the Great – the Rome-appointed king over Palestine – died. The residents of Sepphoris, led by Judah son of Hezekiah, seized the opportunity to throw off Roman rule. The rebellion was brutally crushed by Varus, the Roman governor of Syria. In AD 6 a man called Judas the Galilean led another rebellion after Rome increased taxes. His movement was also crushed. Galilee was first to fall in the great war against Rome in AD 66–70. Interestingly, Sepphoris would surrender and cooperate with Rome, a decision no doubt inspired partly by the memory of the city's destruction seventy years earlier and partly because the Jewish elites living there preferred the status quo. On the history of Jewish zealotry see Martin Hengel, *The Zealots*. T & T Clark, 1989.

13 John Shelby Spong, *Jesus for the Non-Religious*. HarperCollins, 2007, 25–36.
14 John P. Meier, *A Marginal Jew: rethinking the historical Jesus* [vol.1]. Doubleday, 1991, 317.
15 Mark 3:31–34.
16 John 19:25–27; Acts 1:14.
17 John P. Meier, *A Marginal Jew: rethinking the historical Jesus* [vol.1]. Doubleday, 1991, 317. See also the work of the great Jewish scholar David Flusser, 'Jesus, His Ancestry and the Commandment to Love' in James Charlesworth (editor), *Jesus' Jewishness*. Crossroad, 1991 (153–176), 160.
18 See too John P. Meier, *A Marginal Jew: rethinking the historical Jesus* [vol.1]. Doubleday, 1991, 227. The point may be dulled by the fact that Matthew changes the wording to 'Isn't this the carpenter's son? Isn't his mother's name Mary…?' (Matthew 13:55) and Luke has 'Isn't this Joseph's son?' (Luke 4:22). John 1:45 has Jesus described as 'Jesus of Nazareth, the son of Joseph'. Nevertheless, it remains true that the earliest description (Mark's), neglects to mention Jesus' father by name.
19 *Jewish Antiquities* 20.200. The translation is that of Louis H. Feldman (Loeb Classical Library vol.456. Harvard University Press, 1996).
20 See the judicious survey of the history of interpretation of Jesus' 'brothers/sisters' in John P. Meier, *A Marginal Jew: rethinking the historical Jesus* [vol.1]. Doubleday, 1991, 317–332.
21 The doctrine of the perpetual virginity of Mary was first proposed in a document known as the *Protevangelium of James* (late second century) and championed as true dogma by St Jerome in his tract *Against Helvidius* (late fourth century).
22 While doubted by past scholarship, there is growing agreement amongst scholars that the letter of James did indeed derive from the brother of Jesus and leader of the earliest Christians in Jerusalem. See Peter H. Davids' superb study, *The Epistle of James*. Eerdmans, 1982, 1–61. Others prefer to argue that the core teaching of the epistle came from James, the brother of Jesus, but that it was put into its final epistolary form by a disciple of James. For example, see Ralph P. Martin, *James* (Word Biblical Commentary, vol.48). Thomas Nelson, 1988, xxxi–lxxvii.
23 Acts 21:18–25; Galatians 2:9.
24 1 Corinthians 9:5.

25 Richard Bauckham, *Jude and the Relatives of Jesus in the Early Church*. T & T Clark, 1990, 57–70.
26 The source of the theory in recent times is Dan Brown, *The Da Vinci Code*. Bantam Press, 2003, 245–249. A more serious attempt to argue that Jesus was married is William E. Phipps, *Was Jesus Married? The Distortion of Sexuality in the Christian Tradition*. Harper & Row, 1970. His argument is gentlemanly demolished by John P. Meier, *A Marginal Jew*, vol.1. Doubleday, 1991, 332–345; 363–365.
27 Gospel of Philip 55. The translation is that of Hans-Martin Schenke in *New Testament Apocrypha, Volume. 1: Gospels and Related Writings* (edited by Wilhelm Schneemelcher). James Clarke & Co. Ltd, 1991, 194.
28 'Greet one another with a kiss of love' (1 Peter 5:14).
29 Josephus mentions the Essenes' practice of celibacy but makes clear that they do not condemn wedlock in principle (Josephus, *Jewish War* 2.121).
30 Jeremiah 16:2–4.
31 See the comprehensive discussion in John P. Meier, *A Marginal Jew*, vol.1. Doubleday, 1991, 332–345; 363–365.
32 The source of the Eastern sojourn account of Jesus' missing years was the 1894 book by Russian journalist Nicholas Notovitch. It was exposed as a hoax shortly after its publication but, still, new editions appear: Nicholas Notovitch, *The Unknown Life of Jesus Christ*. Dragon Key Press, 2002.
33 David Flusser, 'Jesus, His Ancestry and the Commandment to Love' in James Charlesworth (editor), *Jesus' Jewishness*. Crossroad, 1991 (153–176), 162.
34 Mark 6:3; then repeated in Matthew 13:55.
35 See the commonsense discussion in John P. Meier, *A Marginal Jew: rethinking the historical Jesus* [vol.1]. Doubleday, 1991, 278–285.
36 John P. Meier, *A Marginal Jew: rethinking the historical Jesus* [vol.1]. Doubleday, 1991, 281.

CHAPTER 4. MENTOR AND COMPETITORS

1 For example Rainer Riesner, *Jesus als Lehrer* [trans. *Jesus as Teacher]*. Mohr Siebeck, 1981 [not yet translated into English]; Pheme Perkins, *Jesus as Teacher*. Cambridge University Press, 1990.

2 Mohandas K. Gandhi, *Autobiography: The Story of My Experiments with Truth*. Dover Publications, 1983, 60. His full name was Mohandas Karamchand Gandhi. 'Mahatma' is a title of affection meaning Great Soul.
3 Richard Dawkins, *The God Delusion*. Bantam Press, 2006, 340–344. Dawkins believes that 'literary education' is where the value of the Bible begins and ends.
4 Josephus, *Jewish Antiquities* 18.116–119. The translation is that of Louis H. Feldman (Loeb Classical Library vol.433. Harvard University Press, 1996).
5 Josephus, *Life* 11–12.
6 The Greek word *metanoia*, 'repent', combines the words *meta* ('change') and *noia/nous* (mind) and refers to more than a 'change of form' – *metamorphosis* in Greek. *Metanoia* refers to a fundamental change in attitude that expresses itself in changed behaviours; hence the Baptist's call to 'produce fruit in keeping with repentance'.
7 Dale C. Allison, *Jesus of Nazareth: Millenarian Prophet*. Fortress Press, 1998, 104–105; Craig A. Evans, 'Context, Family and Formation' (11–24) in *The Cambridge Companion to Jesus* (edited by Marcus Bockmuehl). Cambridge University Press, 2001, 21; James Dunn, *Jesus Remembered*. Eerdmans, 2003, 141; Kurt Rudolph, 'The Baptist Sects' (471–500) in *The Cambridge History of Judaism (vol.3): the Early Roman Period* (edited by William Horbury *et al.*). Cambridge University Press, 2001, 495–497; James Dunn, *Jesus Remembered*. Eerdmans, 2003, 350–352; Graham Stanton, *The Gospels and Jesus* (Second Edition). Oxford University Press, 2003, 184–189.
8 The relevant data are: (1) the Baptist's ministry predates that of Jesus; (2) Jesus submits himself to the Baptist's unique ritual; (3) some of Jesus' central ideas are the same as those of the Baptist; (4) two or three of Jesus' disciples come out of the circle of the Baptist; (5) Jesus praises the Baptist as the greatest man/prophet in Israel's history; (6) Jesus and his disciples continue to practise the Baptist's defining ritual. All in all, this convinces most (including me) that Jesus started out under the influence of John the Baptist.
9 Paula Fredriksen, *Jesus of Nazareth: King of the Jews*. Vintage Books, 1997, 191.
10 Mark 1:9. The episode is repeated in Matthew 3:13 and Luke 3:21, though not in John's Gospel. Because the Gospel writers would have no reason to invent a story about Jesus submitting to John in this way – and every reason to skip over it – scholars universally agree

that Jesus' baptism by John is historical. This is an example of what scholars call the *criterion of embarrassment*: details that are likely to be embarrassing to the early Christians but are reported anyway are highly likely to be credible.

11 John 3:22, 26; 4:2.

12 John 1:35–42 makes clear that Andrew and another unnamed disciple were John's disciples first. Andrew was the brother of the famous apostle Peter. Was Peter also a former disciple of John? Peter and Andrew were both from Capernaum on the northern tip of Lake Galilee. Given that the Baptist operated much further south, we can see here just how far-reaching his ministry was. There is no historical difficulty imagining that Jesus, who grew up near Capernaum and based much of his ministry there, also felt the powerful influence of John.

13 A classic example is John P. Meier, *A Marginal Jew* (vol.2). Doubleday, 1994, 19–233.

14 Matthew 11:2–3 | Luke 7:18–20.

15 Mark 1:7–8 (repeated in Matthew 3:11 and Luke 3:16) and John 1:26–27.

16 On the origin of the Pharisees see Joachim Schaper, 'The Pharisees' (402–427) in *The Cambridge History of Judaism (vol.3): the Early Roman Period* (edited by William Horbury *et al.*). Cambridge University Press, 2001.

17 Josephus, *Jewish War* 2.162.

18 Mishnah *Abot* 1.15. The translation comes from Jacob Neusner, *The Mishnah: A New Translation*. Yale University Press, 1988.

19 Mishnah *Abot* 1.12. The translation comes from Jacob Neusner, *The Mishnah: A New Translation*. Yale University Press, 1988.

20 Mishnah *Gittin* 9.10 lists the ancient rabbis' rulings on divorce. Jesus' own views are found in Matthew 5:32; Mark 10:11; Luke 16:18.

21 On the authenticity of this tradition see James Dunn, *Jesus Remembered*. Eerdmans, 2003, 570–572.

22 Mishnah *Yadayim* 2.3. The translation comes from Jacob Neusner, *The Mishnah: A New Translation*. Yale University Press, 1988.

23 This is reported in Mishnah *Yadayim* 3.5.

CHAPTER 5. KINGDOM OF JUDGEMENT AND LOVE

1 A blatant example of this modern co-opting of a 'liberal Jesus' is Bishop John Shelby Spong's *Jesus for the Non-Religious*. HarperCollins,

2007 (especially chapters 22–24). But there are scholarly versions as well. See, for example, John Dominic Crossan, *The Historical Jesus*. Harper San Francisco, 1991.

2 Examples from Q include: Luke 11:20 | Matthew 12:28; Luke 6:20 | Matthew 5:3; Luke 7:28 | Matthew 11:11; Luke 9:2 | Matthew 10:7; Luke 13:20 | Matthew 13:33; Luke 13:28–29 | Matthew 8:11; Luke 16:16 | Matthew 11:12. In the Gospel of Mark we find the following: Mark 4:11, 26, 30; 9:1, 47; 10:14, 23, 24; 14:25. In L and M we find a few more examples: Luke 9:62; 17:20–21; Matthew 5:19; 13:43, 44, 47, 52; 18:23; 25:1, 34.

3 In the Old Testament see: Psalm 145:8–13; Isaiah 52:7. The theme also emerges in the *Psalms of Solomon*, a non-scriptural Jewish text written shortly before Jesus. Chapter 17 of the document has a full-scale vision of the establishment of God's kingdom. The Dead Sea Scrolls also contain references to the coming kingdom: *The War Scroll* (1QM) 6.6; 19.1–8. A curious difference between Jesus' vision of the kingdom and that found in these texts is the way he says nothing about God's judgement on Gentiles. For Jesus, it is Israel that is under judgement, whereas in *Psalms of Solomon* 17 and *War Scroll* 19 it is foreigners who fare worst in the kingdom. For further information on the theme of the kingdom of God see the massive scholarly discussion in John P. Meier, *A Marginal Jew* (vol.2). Doubleday, 1994, 237–506.

4 Dale C. Allison, *Jesus of Nazareth: Millenarian Prophet*. Fortress Press, 1998, 46 (footnote 142).

5 A passage from Q: Luke 11:42–53 | Matthew 23:1–36.

6 Luke 6:20–26; Luke 16:19–31. The first passage is from Q; the second from L.

7 A passage from Q: Luke 6:37 | Matthew 7:1.

8 The same saying, which is from Q, appears in two different contexts: Luke 13:28–30 | Matthew 8:11–12.

9 Mark 13:1–2; Q (Luke 13:34–35 | Matthew 23:37–38) and John 2:19.

10 A passage from Q: Matthew 11:21–24 | Luke 10:12–15.

11 Israel is depicted as a vineyard in Isaiah 5:3–7.

12 Matthew 7:24–27 | Luke 6:47–49; Matthew 13:24–30; 47–48; 25:31–46; Luke 12:16–20; 16:19–31.

13 The Q passage quoted earlier (Luke 7:34 | Matthew 11:19).

14 In Q, Luke 6:27–28 | Matthew 5:44; in Mark 12:28–31; in L, Luke 10:25–30; in 1 John 4:21; and many others.

15 Mishnah *Abot* 1.12.

16 Testament of Issachar 5.1–3. The translation is that of Howard C. Kee in *The Old Testament Pseudepigrapha* vol.1 (edited by James Charlesworth). Doubleday, 1983.
17 Vermes has expressed similar thoughts, albeit a little less enthusiastically, in print as well: Geza Vermes, *The Authentic Gospel of Jesus*. Penguin, 2003, 196–198, 351.
18 David Flusser, 'Jesus, His Ancestry and the Commandment to Love' (153–176) in *Jesus' Jewishness* (edited by James Charlesworth). Crossroad, 1991, 165.
19 Josephus, *Jewish Antiquities* 17.288–289.
20 Josephus, *Jewish Antiquities* 18.4–10, 23–25.
21 Josephus, *Jewish War* 2.433–448.
22 Josephus, *Jewish War* 7.252–401.
23 We see this already in *Psalms of Solomon* 17, written in Jerusalem in the middle of the first century BC.
24 Richard Dawkins, *The God Delusion*. Bantam, 2006, 253, 257.
25 Rodney Stark, *The Rise of Christianity*. HarperCollins, 1997, 209–215.

CHAPTER 6. STRANGE CIRCLE OF FRIENDS

1 Josephus, *Jewish Antiquities* 18.64.
2 Talmud, *baraitha Sanhedrin* 43a.
3 For a recent scholarly treatment of the small differences between the various lists of twelve apostles, see Richard Bauckham, *Jesus and the Eyewitnesses*. Eerdmans, 2006, 93–113.
4 In the Old Testament see Genesis 49:28; Exodus 24:4; Numbers 17:2; Ezra 8:35. In the New Testament see James 1:1 and Revelation 21:12.
5 John Shelby Spong, *Jesus for the Non-Religious*. HarperCollins, 2007, 37–47.
6 The twelve are attested in Mark (3:14; 4:10; 6:7; 9:35; 10:32; 11:11; 14:10), in Q (Matthew 19:28 | Luke 22:29–30), John (6:70; 20:24), Paul (1 Corinthians 15:5) and in L (Luke 6:13–16; Acts 1:13).
7 E. P. Sanders, *The Historical Figure of Jesus*. Penguin Books, 1993, 253.
8 Hosea 1:2–9.
9 Ezekiel 4:1–13.
10 Graham Stanton, *The Gospels and Jesus* (Second Edition). Oxford University Press, 2003, 201.

11 Graham Stanton, *The Gospels and Jesus* (Second Edition). Oxford University Press, 2003, 201–202.
12 John Shelby Spong, *Jesus for the Non-Religious*. HarperCollins, 2007. See especially pages 256–262.
13 Paula Fredriksen, *Jesus of Nazareth: King of the Jews*. Vintage Books, 1997, 201–202. A similar caution is sounded by Richard Bauckham, *Gospel Women: Studies in the Named Women in the Gospels*. Eerdmans, 2002, xi–xvii.
14 The prices of ancient goods are listed in David Hendin, *Guide to Biblical Coins* (Fourth Edition). Amphora, 2001, 37–38.
15 John P. Meier, *A Marginal Jew: rethinking the historical Jesus* [vol.3]. Doubleday, 2001, 76.
16 James Dunn, *Jesus Remembered*. Eerdmans, 2003, 535; E. P. Sanders, *The Historical Figure of Jesus*. Penguin Books, 1993, 109–111.
17 Mark 16:1–8; Luke 24:1–12; Matthew 28:1–8; John 20:1–13.
18 Ben F. Meyer, *The Aims of Jesus*. SCM, 1979, 158.
19 *Psalms of Solomon* 15.8–10.
20 *Psalms of Solomon* 17.21–32.
21 Graham Stanton, 'Message and Miracles' in *The Cambridge Companion to Jesus*. Cambridge University Press, 2001, 69; likewise James Dunn, *Jesus Remembered*. Eerdmans, 2003, 599–605; Joachim Jeremias, *New Testament Theology (vol.1): The Proclamation of Jesus*. SCM, 1971, 115–116.
22 Ben Sira 9.16; 11.29; 1QS (*The Community Rule*) 6.24; Josephus, *Jewish War* 2.129–144.
23 Luke 7:34 | Matthew 11:19.
24 Craig L. Blomberg, *Contagious Holiness: Jesus' meals with sinners*. IVP, 2005.

CHAPTER 7. MIRACLES, HISTORY AND THE KINGDOM

1 An extreme example is the twenty-page preamble 'Miracles and Modern Minds' in John P. Meier, *A Marginal Jew: Rethinking the Historical Jesus* (vol.2). Doubleday, 1994, 509–534. Similar introductions are found in Marcus J. Borg, *Jesus: A New Vision: Spirit, Culture, and the Life of Discipleship*. HarperCollins, 1991, 57–60; E. P. Sanders, *The Historical Figure of Jesus*. Penguin Books, 1993, 132–135; Gerd Theissen and Annette Merz, *The Historical Jesus: a comprehensive guide*. Fortress Press, 1998, 281–282.
2 Josephus, *Jewish Antiquities* 18.63.

3 James Dunn, *Jesus Remembered*. Eerdmans, 2003, 670.
4 John Shelby Spong, *Jesus for the Non-Religious*. HarperCollins, 2007, 84.
5 Paula Fredriksen, *Jesus of Nazareth: King of the Jews*. Vintage Books, 1997, 114; John Dominic Crossan, *Jesus: A Revolutionary Biography*. HarperSanFransisco, 1994, 82, 85, 91–93.
6 The most comprehensive historical study of the topic is currently the 500-page treatment in John P. Meier, *A Marginal Jew: Rethinking the Historical Jesus* (vol.2). Doubleday, 1994, 509–1038.
7 The other passage is Matthew 11:2–6 | Luke 7:18–23.
8 Mark 3:22–23; John 8:48–53.
9 Talmud *b. Sanhedrin* 43a.
10 Gerd Theissen and Annette Merz, *The Historical Jesus: a comprehensive guide*. Fortress Press, 1998, 309.
11 Richard Dawkins, *The God Delusion*. Bantam Press, 2006, 91–92.
12 Dawkins' argument is really a rerun of the one offered by the famous eighteenth-century Scottish philosopher David Hume in his chapter 'Of Miracles' in *On Human Nature and the Understanding*. Macmillan, 1962, 115–136. A host of books critiquing Hume's objection to miracles have been written by professional philosophers: J. C. A. Gaskin, *Hume's Philosophy of Religion*. Macmillan, 1978 (Chapter 7 especially); F. J. Beckwith, *David Hume's Argument Against Miracles: A Critical Analysis*. University Press of America, 1989; M. P. Levine, *Hume and The Problem of Miracles: A Solution*. Kluwer, 1989; J. Houston, *Reported Miracles: A Critique of Hume*. Cambridge University Press, 1994; J. Earman, *Hume's Abject Failure: The Argument Against Miracles*. Oxford University Press, 2000.
13 John P. Meier, *A Marginal Jew: Rethinking the Historical Jesus* (vol.2). Doubleday, 1994, 514.

CHAPTER 8. CONTRA JERUSALEM

1 2 Samuel 5:3–13.
2 Graham Stanton, *The Gospels and Jesus* (Second Edition). Oxford University Press, 2003, 276.
3 Deuteronomy 16:16.
4 Zechariah 9:9.
5 E. P. Sanders, *The Historical Figure of Jesus*. Penguin Books, 1993, 253–254; see also his *Jesus and Judaism*. Fortress Press, 1985,

306–308; Marcus J. Borg, *Jesus: a New Vision: Spirit, Culture, and the Life of Discipleship*. HarperCollins, 1991, 173–174.

6 Marcus J. Borg, *Jesus: a New Vision: Spirit, Culture, and the Life of Discipleship*. HarperCollins, 1991, 174.

7 E. P. Sanders, *The Historical Figure of Jesus*. Penguin Books, 1993, 254.

8 For a detailed description of the Temple's size and layout see E. P. Sanders, *Judaism: Practice & Belief, 63* BCE*–66* CE. SCM Press, 1992, 55–69. The best ancient source (supplemented by archaeology) is, once again, Josephus, *The Jewish War* 5.184–227.

9 *Psalms of Solomon* 4.20–22; 8.11; and from the Dead Sea Scrolls, 1QpHab 8.8–12; 9.3–6.

10 See, for example, *Christ cleansing the Temple* by El Greco (Domenikos Theotokopoulos; 1541–1614); and one with the same title by Luca Giordano (1632–1705).

11 These words come back to bite Jesus at his trial. See Mark 14:57–58; repeated in Matthew 26:61.

12 A passage from Q: Luke 11:42–53 | Matthew 23:1–36. See also Luke 6:20–26; 16:19–31.

13 A passage from Q: Matthew 11:21–24 | Luke 10:12–15.

14 Mark 13:1–2 contains another statement about the destruction of the Temple (it is repeated in Matthew 24:1–2 and Luke 21:5–6).

15 Sean Freyne, *Jesus, a Jewish Galilean: A New Reading of the Jesus-Story*. T & T Clark, 2005, 122–170.

16 Josephus, *The Jewish War* 6.252–281. The translation is that of H. ST. J. Thackeray (Loeb Classical Library vol. 487. Harvard University Press, 1997).

CHAPTER 9. LAST SUPPER

1 To list just a few: James Dunn, *Jesus Remembered*. Eerdmans, 2003, 796–804; E. P. Sanders, *The Historical Figure of Jesus*. Penguin Books, 1993, 263–264; Gerd Theissen and Annette Merz, *The Historical Jesus: a comprehensive guide*. Fortress Press, 1998, 436–437; Graham Stanton, *The Gospels and Jesus* (Second Edition). Oxford University Press, 2003, 274–279.

2 The Old Testament prophets believed in Jesus' day to have suffered martyrdom include Isaiah, Jeremiah, Amos and Micah.

3 See also two more passages from Q (Matthew 5:12 | Luke 6:23; and Matthew 23:37 | Luke 13:34).

4 E. P. Sanders, *The Historical Figure of Jesus*. Penguin Books, 1993, 263.
5 The requirements for the Passover sacrifice are laid out in Mishnah *Pesahim* 5.1 – 6.2.
6 Richard Dawkins, *The God Delusion*. Bantam Press, 2006, 253.
7 Martin Hengel, *The Atonement: The Origins of the Doctrine in the New Testament*. Wipf & Stock, 1981.
8 Bernd Janowski and Peter Stuhlmacher (editors), *The Suffering Servant: Isaiah 53 in Jewish and Christian Sources*. Eerdmans, 2004. Years earlier the significance of Isaiah 53 for the Christian understanding of Jesus' death was examined by Joachim Jeremias, *New Testament Theology (vol.1): The Proclamation of Jesus*. SCM, 1971, 286–288.
9 Martin Hengel, *The Atonement: The Origins of the Doctrine in the New Testament*. Wipf & Stock, 2007, 72.

CHAPTER 10. CRUCIFIXION

1 John Shelby Spong, *Jesus for the Non-Religious*. HarperCollins, 2007, 115.
2 The exception is the idiosyncratic John Dominic Crossan, *The Historical Jesus*. HarperSanFrancisco, 1991, 372. See the excellent – very polite – review of Crossan in Mark Allan Powell, *Jesus as a Figure of History: How Modern Historians View the Man from Galilee*. Westminster John Knox Press, 1998, 65–99.
3 The eyewitnesses referred to are: Peter (Mark 14:66–71; repeated in Matthew 26:69–74 and Luke 22:56–60; independently in John 18:25–27), Simon of Cyrene (Mark 15:20–24; repeated in Matthew 27:31–32 and Luke 23:26) and the women disciples (Mark 15:40–41; repeated in Matthew 27:55–56 and Luke 23:49; independently in John 19:25–27). On this see Richard Bauckham, *Jesus and the Eyewitnesses*. Eerdmans, 2006, 48–52; James Dunn, *Jesus Remembered*. Eerdmans, 2003, 779.
4 'Naming the conflict. "The War to Return the Captives" is leading contender', *Jerusalem Post*, 19 March 2007. The biblical allusions are many: Deuteronomy 30:3; Isaiah 42:7; 61:1; Amos 9:14 (where in Hebrew the phrase is precisely 'return the captives').
5 Two leading names from the sceptical end of mainstream scholarship will provide readers with a clear picture of this scholarly consensus about the passion narratives: E. P. Sanders, *Jesus and*

Judaism. Fortress Press, 1985, 294–318; Marcus J. Borg, *Jesus: a New Vision: Spirit, Culture, and the Life of Discipleship*. HarperCollins, 1991, 178–184.

6 See, for example, E. P. Sanders, *Jesus and Judaism*. Fortress Press, 1985, 296–306; Gerd Theissen and Annette Merz, *The Historical Jesus: a comprehensive guide*. Fortress Press, 1998, 465; Graham Stanton, *The Gospels and Jesus* (Second Edition). Oxford University Press, 2003, 285; Marcus J. Borg, *Jesus: A New Vision: Spirit, Culture, and the Life of Discipleship*. HarperCollins, 1991, 180–183; Joachim Jeremias, *New Testament Theology (vol. 1): The Proclamation of Jesus*. SCM, 1971, 279–280.

7 E. P. Sanders, *Jesus and Judaism*. Fortress Press, 1985, 305.

8 Zechariah 9:9.

9 See E. P. Sanders, *Judaism: Practice & Belief, 63 BCE–66 CE*. SCM Press, 1992, 137–138. Josephus records that during one Passover thousands of worshippers were killed by the Romans for starting a riot: Josephus, *Jewish Antiquities* 20.106–112.

10 The definitive history of crucifixion and its relevance to the death of Jesus was written years ago by Martin Hengel, *Crucifixion: In the ancient world and the folly of the message of the cross*. Fortress Press, 1977.

11 Michel Onfray, *Atheist Manifesto*. Arcade Publishing, 2005, 128.

12 Richard Dawkins, *The God Delusion*. Bantam Press, 2006, 251.

13 James Dunn, *Jesus Remembered*. Eerdmans, 2003, 855.

CHAPTER 11. RESURRECTION

1 Honi got the nickname 'Circle-drawer' after praying for rain during a drought. He drew a circle around himself and told God that he would not leave the spot until rain fell. Apparently, it soon did.

2 Josephus, *Jewish Antiquities* 14.22–24.

3 Orthodox Jews find the names Hillel and Shammai in their Mishnah but the Orthodox are a minority today.

4 Craig A. Evans, *Life of Jesus Research: An Annotated Bibliography*. Brill, 1989, 151–162.

5 Stephen T. Davis (editor), *The Resurrection: An Interdisciplinary Symposium on the Resurrection of Jesus*. Oxford University Press, 1998.

6 A classic example of Christian apologetics on the resurrection is William Lane Craig, *The Son Rises: The Historical Evidence for the Resurrection of Jesus*. Wipf & Stock, 2000. It is actually very, very good. Nevertheless, I am not utilizing such works in this chapter.

7 Graham Stanton, *The Gospels and Jesus* (Second Edition). Oxford University Press, 2003, 288–291; James Dunn, *Jesus Remembered.* Eerdmans, 2003, 825–879; Gerd Theissen and Annette Merz, *The Historical Jesus: a comprehensive guide.* Fortress Press, 1998, 474–511; Marcus Bockmuehl, 'Resurrection' (102–118) in *The Cambridge Companion to Jesus* (edited by Marcus Bockmuehl). Cambridge University Press, 2001; E. P. Sanders, *The Historical Figure of Jesus.* Penguin Books, 1993, 276–281.
8 E. P. Sanders, *The Historical Figure of Jesus.* Penguin Books, 1993, 280.
9 N. T. Wright, *The Resurrection of the Son of God.* SPCK, 2003, 718.
10 John Shelby Spong, *Jesus for the Non-Religious.* HarperCollins, 2007, 117–129. Spong dismisses the empty tomb stories on the grounds that the proper burial of crucified criminals was 'all but unknown' (120). This is contradicted by numerous ancient sources (Philo, *Flaccus* 83; Josephus, *Jewish War* 4.317) and by the discovery in 1968 of the remains of a crucified man *in a family tomb*. Spong further insists that the apostle Paul – our earliest written source – knew nothing about any tomb. He overlooks the fact that saying a person 'was buried' (as Paul says of Jesus in 1 Corinthians 15:4) can, for a Jew, mean nothing other than that he was properly buried, making it likely that Paul did know something of Jesus' tomb. As for Spong's claim that the New Testament resurrection reports are intended to be metaphorical expressions of the transcendent realization that even death could not destroy the Christ-experience, this owes more to trends in literature and theology than to historical method.
11 Representative of the mainstream scholarly discussion of these two matters is Graham Stanton, *The Gospels and Jesus* (Second Edition). Oxford University Press, 2003, 288–291. A more detailed examination is found in James Dunn, *Jesus Remembered.* Eerdmans, 2003, 828–841.
12 James Dunn, *Jesus Remembered.* Eerdmans, 2003, 861–862.
13 For example, G. Lüdemann, *What Really Happened to Jesus. A Historical Approach to the Resurrection.* Westminster John Knox Press, 1995, 14–15; R. Funk, *The Acts of Jesus: The Search for the Authentic Deeds of Jesus.* HarperSanFrancisco, 1998, 466.
14 Acts 1:26.
15 James Dunn, *Jesus Remembered.* Eerdmans, 2003, 832–833. The first-century Jewish historian Josephus remarks, 'From women let no evidence be accepted, because of the levity and temerity of their

sex' (Josephus, *Jewish Antiquities* 4.219). Likewise the ancient Jewish legal code, the Mishnah, stipulates: 'The law governing an oath of testimony applies to men and not to women, to those who are suitable to bear witness and not to those who are unsuitable to bear witness' (Mishnah *Shabuot* 4.1).

16 Graham Stanton, *The Gospels and Jesus*. Oxford University Press, 2003, 289–290.

17 The mid-second-century critic of Christianity, Celsus, wryly stated, 'after death he rose again and showed the marks of his punishment and how his hands had been pierced. But who saw this? A hysterical female' (Origen, *Contra Celsum* 2.55).

18 For scholarly accounts of these issues, see Richard Bauckham, *Gospel Women: Studies in the Named Women in the Gospels*. Eerdmans, 2002, 268–277; James Dunn, *Jesus Remembered*. Eerdmans, 2003, 832–833; Graham Stanton, *The Gospels and Jesus* (Second Edition). Oxford University Press, 2003, 289–290; N. T. Wright, *The Resurrection of the Son of God*. SPCK, 2003, 607–608; Gerd Theissen and Annette Merz, *The Historical Jesus: a comprehensive guide*. Fortress Press, 1998, 495–499.

19 E. P. Sanders, *The Historical Figure of Jesus*. Penguin Books, 1993, 280.

EPILOGUE. A SHORT LIFE?

1 Paula Fredriksen, *Jesus of Nazareth: King of the Jews*. Vintage Books, 1997, 201–202.

2 Graham Stanton, *The Gospels and Jesus* (Second Edition). Oxford University Press, 2003, 176–177, 296–299; E. P. Sanders, *Jesus and Judaism*. Fortress Press, 1985, 3, 18–22.

3 E. P. Sanders, *Jesus and Judaism*. Fortress Press, 1985, 340.

4 The book of Acts provides evidence that the Temple was still viewed by the early believers in Jesus as a place of prayer and teaching (as it had been for Jesus): Acts 3:1–10; 5:25, 42; 21:26–30.

5 James 1:25.

6 Mark 7:1–8.

7 Galatians 5:6.

8 A key passage in Acts 15.

9 Galatians 3:28.

10 E. P. Sanders, *Jesus and Judaism*. Fortress Press, 1985, 39–40, 200–202.

11 Mark 2:7.
12 1 Corinthians 15:3.
13 E. P. Sanders, *The Historical Figure of Jesus*. Penguin Books, 1993, 11.
14 Matthew 6:10.
15 Graham Stanton, *The Gospels and Jesus* (Second Edition). Oxford University Press, 2003, 296–297.
16 The leader in this particular field is Professor Larry Hurtado of the University of Edinburgh. An accessible version of his research is found in *How on Earth Did Jesus Become a God? Historical Questions about Earliest Devotion to Jesus*. Eerdmans, 2005.
17 Graham Stanton, *The Gospels and Jesus* (Second Edition). Oxford University Press, 2003, 297.
18 E. P. Sanders, *Jesus and Judaism*. Fortress Press, 1985, 307.
19 This is the key finding of Larry Hurtado, *How on Earth Did Jesus Become a God? Historical Questions about Earliest Devotion to Jesus*. Eerdmans, 2005, 179–206.
20 Romans 7:2–4; 2 Corinthians 11:2; Ephesians 5:25–32; Revelation 19:7; 21:9.

SELECT BIBLIOGRAPHY

Achtemeier, P. J., Green, J. B. and Thomson, M. M. (editors), *Introducing the New Testament: Its Literature and Theology*. Eerdmans, 2001.

Akenson, D. H., *Saint Saul: A Skeleton Key to the Historical Jesus*. Oxford University Press, 2000.

Alexander, L., 'What is a gospel?' (13–33) in *The Cambridge Companion to the Gospels* (edited by S. C. Barton). Cambridge University Press, 2006.

Alexander, P. S., 'Jesus and the Golden Rule' (363–388) in *Hillel and Jesus: Comparative Studies of Two Major Religious Leaders* (edited by J. H. Charlesworth and L. L. Johns). Fortress Press, 1997.

Allison, D. C., *Jesus of Nazareth: Millenarian Prophet*. Fortress Press, 1998.

Archer, J., *The Gospel According to Judas, by Benjamin Iscariot*. Macmillan, 2007.

Bauckham, R., *Jude and the Relatives of Jesus in the Early Church*. T & T Clark, 1990.

Bauckham, R., *Gospel Women: Studies in the Named Women in the Gospels*. Eerdmans, 2002.

Bauckham, R., *Jesus and the Eyewitnesses: The Gospels as Eyewitness Testimony*. Eerdmans, 2006.

Bauckham, R., 'James and the Jerusalem Community' (55–95) in *Jewish Believers in Jesus: The Early Centuries* (edited by O. Skarsaune and R. Hvalvik). Hendrickson, 2007.

Beckwith, F. J., *David Hume's Argument Against Miracles: A Critical Analysis*. University Press of America, 1989.

Betz, O., 'The Essenes' (444–470) in *The Cambridge History of Judaism (vol.3): the Early Roman Period* (edited by W. Horbury *et al.*). Cambridge University Press, 2001.

Blomberg, C. L., *Contagious Holiness: Jesus' meals with sinners*. IVP, 2005.

Borg, M. J., *Jesus: A New Vision: Spirit, Culture, and the Life of Discipleship*. HarperCollins, 1991.

Bornkam, G., *Jesus of Nazareth*. Hodder and Stoughton, 1960.

Bowker, J. (editor), *The Oxford Dictionary of World Religions*. Oxford University Press, 1999.

Brakke, D., 'The Gnostics and their opponents' (245–260) in *The Cambridge History of Christianity: Origins to Constantine* (edited by M. M. Mitchell and

F. M. Yong). Cambridge University Press, 2006.

Brown, D., *The Da Vinci Code*. Bantam Press, 2003.

Brown, R. E., *The Birth of the Messiah.* Cassell & Collier Macmillan, 1977.

Brown, R. E., *The Death of the Messiah: From Gethsemane to the Grave* (in two volumes). Doubleday, 1994.

Bultmann, R., *The History of the Synoptic Tradition.* Blackwell, 1972. The original German edition was published in 1921.

Burridge, R., *What are the Gospels? A Comparison With Graeco-Roman Biography*. Cambridge University Press, 1992.

Byrskog, S., *Story as History, History as Story: The Gospel Tradition in the Context of Ancient Oral History.* Brill Academic Publishers, 2002.

Charlesworth, J. H., *Jesus Within Judaism: New Light From Exciting Archaeological Discoveries*. Doubleday, 1988.

Charlesworth, J. H. (editor), *Jesus' Jewishness: Exploring the Place of Jesus within Early Judaism.* Crossroad Publishing, 1991.

Charlesworth, J. H., 'The Dead Sea Scrolls and the historical Jesus' (1–74) in *Jesus and the Dead Sea Scrolls* (edited by J. H. Charlesworth). Doubleday, 1992.

Chilton, B., *Rabbi Jesus: An Intimate Biography.* Doubleday, 2000.

Chin, C. M., 'Rhetorical Practice in the Chreia Elaboration of Mara bar Serapion', *Hugoye: Journal of Syriac Studies*, Vol.9, No.2 (July 2006), 21.

Craig, W. L., *The Son Rises: The Historical Evidence for the Resurrection of Jesus.* Wipf & Stock, 2000.

Crossan, J. D., *The Historical Jesus*. Harper San Francisco, 1991.

Crossan, J. D., 'Parable' (146–152) in *The Anchor Bible Dictionary*, vol.5. Doubleday, 1992.

Crossan, J. D., *Jesus: A Revolutionary Biography.* Harper San Francisco, 1994.

Cureton, W., *Spicilegium Syriacum*. London: Francis and John Rivington, 1855, 43–48 (Syriac), 70–76 (English).

Davids, P. H., *The Epistle of James*. Eerdmans, 1982.

Davies, W. D. and Sanders, E. P., 'Jesus: from the Jewish point of view' (618–677) in *The Cambridge History of Judaism (vol.3): The Early Roman Period* (edited by W. Horbury *et al.*). Cambridge University Press, 2001.

Davis, S. T. (editor), *The Resurrection: An Interdisciplinary Symposium on the Resurrection of Jesus*. Oxford University Press, 1998.

Dawkins, R., *The God Delusion*. Bantam Press, 2006.

Dickson, J., *A Spectator's Guide to World Religions: An Introduction to the Big Five.* Blue Bottle Books, 2004.

Dickson, J., *The Christ Files: how historians know what they know about Jesus.* Blue Bottle Books, 2005.

Dickson, J., *James: The Wisdom of the Brother of Jesus.* Aquila Press, 2006.

Dickson, J. P., *Mission-Commitment in Ancient Judaism and in the Pauline Communities.* WUNT II 159. Mohr Siebeck, 2003, 153–177.

Dickson, J. P., 'Gospel as News: euangel - from Aristophanes to the Apostle Paul' in *New Testament Studies* 51. Cambridge University Press (2005), 221–230.

Dungan, D., *A History of the Synoptic Problem.* Doubleday, 1999.

Dunn, J., *Jesus Remembered.* Eerdmans, 2003.

Earman, J., *Hume's Abject Failure: The Argument Against Miracles.* Oxford University Press, 2000.

Evans, C. A., *Life of Jesus Research: An Annotated Bibliography.* Brill, 1989.

Evans, C. A., *Noncanonical Writings and New Testament Interpretation.* Hendrickson, 1992.

Evans, C. S., *The Historical Christ and the Jesus of Faith: The Incarnational Narrative as History.* Clarendon Press, 1996.

Fitzmyer, J. A., *The Semitic Background of the New Testament* (combined edition of *Essays on the Semitic Background of the New Testament* and *A Wandering Aramean: Collected Aramaic Essays*). Eerdmans and Dove, 1997.

Flusser, D., 'Jesus, His Ancestry and the Commandment to Love' (153–176) in *Jesus' Jewishness* (edited by J. Charlesworth). Crossroad, 1991.

Fowl, S. E., 'The gospels and "the historical Jesus"' (76–96) in *The Cambridge Companion to the Gospels* (edited by S. C. Barton). Cambridge University Press, 2006.

France, R. T. and Wenham, D. (editors), *Gospel Perspectives, Volume 3: Studies in Midrash and Historiography.* Wipf & Stock, 2003.

Fredriksen, P., *Jesus of Nazareth: King of the Jews.* Vintage Books, 1997.

Freyne, S., *Jesus, a Jewish Galilean: A New Reading of the Jesus-Story.* T & T Clark, 2005.

Funk, R. and Hoover, R. W. (editors), *The Five Gospels: The Search for the Authentic Words of Jesus.* Macmillan, 1993.

Funk, R., *The Acts of Jesus: The Search for the Authentic Deeds of Jesus.* Harper San Francisco, 1998.

Gabba, E., 'The social, economic and political history of Palestine 63 BCE–CE 70' (94–167) in *The Cambridge History of Judaism (vol.3): The Early Roman Period* (edited by W. Horbury *et al.*). Cambridge University Press, 2001.

Gaskin, J. C. A., *Hume's Philosophy of Religion.* Macmillan, 1978.

Gerhardsson, B., *The Reliability of the Gospel Tradition.* Hendrickson, 2001.

Goulder, M. D., *Midrash and Lection in Matthew.* SPCK, 1974.

Hendin, D., *Guide to Biblical Coins* (Fourth Edition). Amphora, 2001.

Hengel, M., *Judaism and Hellenism: Studies in Their Encounter in Palestine During the Early Hellenistic Period.* Fortress Press, 1975.

Hengel, M., *Crucifixion: In the ancient world and the folly of the message of the cross.* Fortress Press, 1977.

Hengel, M., *The Zealots.* T & T Clark, 1989.

Hengel, M., *The Four Gospels and the One Gospel of Jesus Christ.* Trinity Press, 2000.

Hengel, M. (with Bailey, D. P.), 'The Effective History of Isaiah 53 in the Pre-Christian Period' (75–146) in *The Suffering Servant: Isaiah 53 in Jewish and Christian Sources* (edited by B. Janowski and P. Stuhlmacher). Eerdmans, 2004.

Hengel, M., *The Charismatic Leader and His Followers.* Wipf & Stock, 2005.

Hengel, M., *The Atonement: The Origins of the Doctrine in the New Testament.* Wipf & Stock, 2007.

Hengel, M., *The Son of God: The Origin of Christology and the History of Jewish Hellenistic Religion.* Wipf & Stock, 2007.

Hitchens, C., *God is Not Great: How Religion Poisons Everything.* Twelve, 2007.

Hofius, O., 'The Fourth Servant Song in the New Testament Letters' (163–188) in *The Suffering Servant: Isaiah 53 in Jewish and Christian Sources* (edited by B. Janowski and P. Stuhlmacher). Eerdmans, 2004.

Horsley, R. A. and Silberman, N. A., *The Message and the Kingdom: How Jesus and Paul Ignited a Revolution and Transformed the Ancient World.* Grosset/Putnam, 1997.

Houston, J., *Reported Miracles: A Critique of Hume.* Cambridge University Press, 1994.

Hume, D., 'Of Miracles' (115–136) in *On Human Nature and the Understanding.* Macmillan, 1962.

Hurtado, L., *How on Earth Did Jesus Become a God? Historical Questions about Earliest Devotion to Jesus.* Eerdmans, 2005.

Ilan, T., *Lexicon of Jewish Names in Late Antiquity: Part 1: Palestine 330 BCE–200 CE*. Mohr Siebeck, 2002.

Janowski, J. and Stuhlmacher, P. (editors), *The Suffering Servant: Isaiah 53 in Jewish and Christian Sources*. Eerdmans, 2004.

Jenkins, P., *Hidden Gospels: How the Search for Jesus Lost its Way.* Oxford University Press, 2001.

Jeremias, J., *New Testament Theology (vol. 1): The Proclamation of Jesus*. SCM, 1971.

Johnson, L. T., *The Real Jesus.* HarperCollins, 1996.

Käsemann, E., *Essays on New Testament Themes.* SCM, 1964.

Kee, H. C., *Miracle in the Early Christian World: A Study in Sociohistorical Method.* Yale University Press, 1983.

Kee, H. C., *What Can We Know about Jesus?*. Cambridge University Press, 1990.

Klausner, J., *Jesus of Nazareth: His Life, Times, and Teaching.* Menorah Publishing, 1925.

Lapide, P., *The Resurrection of Jesus: A Jewish Perspective*. Augsburg, 1983.

Levine, M. P., *Hume and the Problem of Miracles: A Solution*. Kluwer, 1989.

Lüdemann, G., *What Really Happened to Jesus: A Historical Approach to the Resurrection.* Westminster John Knox Press, 1995.

Lüdemann, G., *Jesus after Two Thousand Years: What He Really Said and Did.* SCM, 2000.

Meier, J. P., *A Marginal Jew: rethinking the historical Jesus* (in three volumes). Doubleday, 1991–2001.

Metzger, B. M., *The Canon of the New Testament: its origin, development and significance*. Oxford University Press, 1997.

Meyer, B. F., *The Aims of Jesus*. SCM, 1979.

Neusner, J., *From Politics to Piety: The Emergence of Pharisaic Judaism.* Englewood Cliffs, 1973.

Onfray, M., *Atheist Manifesto.* Arcade Publishing, 2005.

Perkins, P., *Jesus as Teacher.* Cambridge University Press, 1990.

Phipps, W. E., *Was Jesus Married? The Distortion of Sexuality in the Christian Tradition.* Harper & Row, 1970.

Pines, S., *An Arabic Version of the Testimonium Flavianum and its Implications*. The Israel Academy of Sciences and Humanities, 1971.

Powell, M. A., *Jesus as a Figure of History: How Modern Historians View the Man from Galilee.* Westminster John Knox Press, 1998.

Prophet, E. C., *The Lost Years of Jesus*. Summit University Press, 1988.

Purvis, J. D., *Jerusalem the Holy City: A Bibliography*. ATLA, 1988.

Riesner, R., 'Synagogues in Jerusalem' in *The Book of Acts in its First Century Setting (vol.4): Palestinian Setting*. Eerdmans, 1995.

Riesner, R., *Paul's Early Period: Chronology, Mission Strategy, Theology*. Eerdmans, 1998.

Rudolph, K., 'Gnosticism' (1033–1044) in *The Anchor Bible Dictionary*, vol.2. Doubleday, 1992.

Rudolph, K., 'The Baptist Sects' (471–500) in *The Cambridge History of Judaism (vol.3): the Early Roman Period* (edited by W. Horbury, *et al*). Cambridge University Press, 2001.

Sanders, E. P., *Jesus and Judaism*. Fortress Press, 1985.

Sanders, E. P., *Judaism: Practice & Belief, 63 BCE–66 CE*. SCM Press, 1992.

Sanders, E. P., *The Historical Figure of Jesus*. Penguin Books, 1993.

Schaper, J., 'The Pharisees' (402–427) in *The Cambridge History of Judaism (vol.3): The Early Roman Period* (edited by W. Horbury *et al.*). Cambridge University Press, 2001.

Schneemelcher, W. (editor), *New Testament Apocrypha* (in two volumes). James Clarke & Co. Ltd, 1991–1992.

Schweitzer, A., *The Quest of the Historical Jesus*. Dover, 2005.

Skarsaune, O. and Hvalvik R. (editors), *Jewish Believers in Jesus: The Early Centuries*. Hendrickson, 2007.

Spong, J. S., *Jesus for the Non-Religious*. HarperCollins, 2007.

Stanton, G., *Jesus of Nazareth in New Testament Preaching*. Cambridge University Press, 1974.

Stanton, G., 'Message and miracles' (56–71) in *The Cambridge Companion to Jesus* (edited by M. Bockmuehl). Cambridge University Press, 2001.

Stanton, G., *The Gospels and Jesus* (Second Edition). Oxford University Press, 2003.

Stark, R., *The Rise of Christianity*. HarperCollins, 1997.

Stuhlmacher, P., *Jesus of Nazareth, Christ of Faith*. Hendrickson, 1993.

Stuhlmacher, P., 'Isaiah 53 in the Gospels and Acts' (147–162) in *The Suffering Servant: Isaiah 53 in Jewish and Christian Sources* (edited by B. Janowski and P. Stuhlmacher). Eerdmans, 2004.

Theissen, G. and Merz, A., *The Historical Jesus: a comprehensive guide*.

Fortress Press, 1998.

Trombley, F., 'Overview: the geographical spread of Christianity' (302–313) in *The Cambridge History of Christianity: Origins to Constantine* (edited by M. M. Mitchell and F. M. Yong). Cambridge University Press, 2006.

Tuckett, C., 'Sources and Methods' (121–137) in *The Cambridge Companion to Jesus* (edited by Marcus Bockmuehl). Cambridge University Press, 2001.

Van Voorst, R., *Jesus Outside the New Testament: An Introduction to the Ancient Evidence.* Eerdmans, 2000.

Vermes, G., *Jesus the Jew: A Historian's Reading of the Gospels.* Collins, 1973.

Vermes, G., *The Authentic Gospel of Jesus.* Penguin, 2003.

von Wahlde, U. C., 'Archaeology and John's Gospel' (523–586) in *Jesus and Archaeology* (edited by J. H. Charlesworth). Eerdmans, 2006.

Wansbrough, H. (editor), *Jesus and the Oral Gospel Tradition.* Sheffield Academic Press, 1991.

Wedderburn, A. J. M., *Beyond Resurrection.* SCM Press, 1999.

Witherington, B., *Women in the Earliest Churches* (Society for New Testament Studies Monograph Series, 58). Cambridge University Press, 1991.

Wolterrstorff, N., *Reason within the Bounds of Religion* (Second Edition). Eerdmans, 1999.

Wright, N. T., *Jesus and the Victory of God.* Fortress Press, 1996.

Wright, N. T., *The Resurrection of the Son of God.* SPCK, 2003.

Wright, N. T., *Judas and the Gospel of Jesus.* SPCK, 2006.

Zias, J. and Charlesworth, J. H., 'Crucifixion: Archaeology, Jesus and the Dead Sea Scrolls' (273–289) in *Jesus and the Dead Sea Scrolls* (edited by J. H. Charlesworth). Doubleday, 1992.

Zias, J. and Sekeles, E., 'The Crucified Man from Giv'at ha-Mivtar: A Reappraisal', *Israel Exploration Journal* 35 (1985), 22–27.

INDEX